Feminist Film Theory and *Cléo from 5 to 7*

FILM THEORY IN PRACTICE

Series Editor: Todd McGowan

FILM THEORY IN PRACTICE

Feminist Film Theory and *Cléo from 5 to 7*

HILARY NERONI

Bloomsbury Academic
An imprint of Bloomsbury Publishing Plc

B L O O M S B U R Y

NEW YORK · LONDON · OXFORD · NEW DELHI · SYDNEY

Bloomsbury Academic

An imprint of Bloomsbury Publishing Inc

1385 Broadway	50 Bedford Square
New York	London
NY 10018	WC1B 3DP
USA	UK

www.bloomsbury.com

BLOOMSBURY and the Diana logo are trademarks of Bloomsbury Publishing Plc

First published 2016

Library of Congress Cataloging-in-Publication Data
Neroni, Hilary, 1969-
Feminist film theory and Cléo from 5 to 7 / Hilary Neroni.
pages cm. – (Film theory in practice)
Includes index.
ISBN 978-1-5013-1368-4 (hardback : alk. paper) –
ISBN 978-1-5013-1369-1 (pbk. : alk. paper) 1. Feminist film criticism.
2. Women in motion pictures. 3. Feminism and motion pictures.
4. Cléo de 5 à 7 (Motion picture)–History and criticism. I. Title.
PN1995.9.W6 N465
791.43'6522 – dc23
2015024517

ISBN: HB: 978-1-5013-1368-4
PB: 978-1-5013-1369-1
ePub: 978-1-5013-1371-4
ePDF: 978-1-5013-1370-7

Series: Film Theory in Practice

Typeset by Integra Software Services Pvt. Ltd.

Printed and bound in the United States of America

to Jane and Del Neroni, truly feminist parents

CONTENTS

Introduction

In 2015, the Cannes Film Festival awarded French filmmaker Agnès Varda an honorary Palme d'Or, the highest honor at the festival. Cannes gives the honorary Palme d'Or as a lifetime achievement award, and Varda was the first female filmmaker to receive the honor, which is not surprising considering the low percentage of women nominated or receiving awards at Cannes. Cannes was aware of this disparity and staged several panels that discussed the plight of women in the film industry that year. Panelists elaborated on the difficulties women face in the industry, including the extremely detrimental effects of male colleagues treating women as sexual objects. Ironically, the Cannes film festival also made the news for another reason. The festival's directors ordered all the ushers to permit only women wearing high heels to enter the site. Following these directions, the ushers barred entrance to female ticket holders wearing flats.

In the same year that the Cannes Film Festival finally awards an honorary Palme d'Or to a female director and sets up panels to address sexism in filmmaking, it also enforces an overtly sexist dress code. This may seem a shocking contradiction, and one might wonder how the festival's directors managed to perform both actions simultaneously. It is a contradiction, but it is one that perfectly encapsulates the contradiction that women face within contemporary society. The festival organizers could perpetuate this contradiction because they live in a society that constantly enacts it. In this sense, the Cannes Film Festival is a symptom of the situation for women today.

Agnès Varda herself would appreciate this contradiction since her films start from the point of contradiction in society and develop a questioning stance from the experience of exploring this contradiction. Varda's questioning stance provides a rich example of the very project of feminism itself, one that the second chapter's analysis of her *Cléo de 5 à 7* (*Cléo from 5 to 7*, 1961) will elucidate. Feminism emerges out of the experience of contradictions like the one evident at the 2015 Cannes Film Festival, and it attempts to force society to confront rather than evade them.

I define feminism through the idea of contradiction. Feminism is the confrontation with the contradictions that surround women, contradictions that stem from the structure of patriarchal society. Though many believe that social progress—women as heads of state, women as corporate executives, woman as major intellectual figures—has obviated the need for feminism in the contemporary world, the fact is that the contradictions surrounding women have become even more pronounced. As equality has made inroads on patriarchy, the pressure on women to conform to an ideal of female beauty has become stronger. Women receive completely contradictory messages today: be powerful and independent on the one hand, but be sexy and perfectly attired on the other. Since feminism begins as a response to the contradictions of the feminine in society, the increasing evidence of these contradictions bespeaks our ever greater need for it. Rather than being the time of the obsolescence of feminism, we exist in a historical moment that calls for its full flowering.

Feminist film theory, which is the subject of this book, develops out of the feminist project and extends its exploration of the contradictions of the feminine to the filmic screen, where these contradictions have manifested themselves since the beginning of cinema. In 1895, the Edison Manufacturing Company's early film *Annabelle Serpentine Dance* depicts the woman as an erotic object, establishing a paradigm that would prevail in cinema up to today. Meanwhile, just a year later, a woman directed what some consider the first fictional film— Alice Guy Blaché's *La Fée aux choux* (1896). From its first moments, cinema turns women into the vehicle for male sexual pleasure, and it gives them an opportunity to communicate a specifically female perspective to a wide audience. This contradiction becomes a recurring concern for feminist film theory.

But because the history of cinema has been primarily doleful for women—because the success of Alice Guy Blaché as a director did not lead to future opportunities for other women—the preoccupation of feminist film theory has been critique. It has taken up the feminist struggle by showing how the structures of popular filmmaking work to enforce sexual inequality. It fights alongside feminist practice, and it often provides an avenue for theorizing what feminist practice leaves unremarked. In what follows, we will see how feminist film theory has made a major contribution to both feminism and to our ability to understand the cinema.

One of the ways feminism makes the contradiction surrounding women evident is to lobby for equality. Discussing the need for equality reshapes the conversation and exposes the inequality at work. Feminism advocates for equality between people in all areas, including economic, political, and social realms. As a movement, feminism arose in the late nineteenth century and early twentieth century in the United States and the United Kingdom in reaction to the contradictions of femininity and the various inequalities women experienced. These included women not having the vote, not having wide spread access to higher education, not having access to many professions, and not having a right to property. By the mid-twentieth century, feminist movements were also pushing for cultural changes as well. People refer to the late nineteenth and early twentieth-century feminist movements as first wave feminism and to the mid-twentieth century movements as second wave feminism.

First wave feminism focused on gaining women's suffrage—the right to vote. This wave of feminism was the longest wave thus far since it took seventy years of struggle to gain the right for women to vote. Women achieved the right to vote in the United States with the passage of the 19th Amendment to the US Constitution in 1920. Most countries granted women the vote during the first half of the twentieth century: for example, France in 1944 and Argentina in 1947. But women in Switzerland did not gain the right to vote until 1971, and women still can't vote in Saudi Arabia and Vatican City.

As in all movements, the suffragists were not unified in their beliefs about how to achieve the vote. Some believed in the power of protest and even hunger strikes, while other groups lobbied politicians and gathered signatures for petitions. Some suffragists infused their protest with theatrical critiques of other restrictive expectations of women. US suffragist Inez Milholland, for example, targeted the tradition of the sidesaddle as a way to protest the right for women to vote when she led a peaceful protest of tens of thousands through New York in 1912, riding astride her horse to the surprise of onlookers. Though first wave feminism focused on the right for women to vote, the impact of the movement was far reaching bringing awareness to issues of equality in all arenas.

It was journalist Marsha Lear who first employed the term "first wave feminism" as she was trying to define the emerging feminism of the late 1960s, which she referred to as a second wave. Her intention was to distinguish the renewed political activity of women in the 1960s from the earlier struggle to gain the vote. Previous to the moniker of "first wave feminism," the struggle to gain the vote was simply referred to as the "suffragist movement." Second wave feminism occurred within the context of the anti-Vietnam War and the Civil Rights movements. It arose during a time of civil protest and social unrest in the United States and around the world.

Second wave feminism addressed social, political, and economic inequalities that barred women from the same opportunities that men had. For example, in the late 1950s in the United States a woman working full time made 59–64 cents for every dollar that their male counterparts made, and it wasn't until the 1963 Equal Pay Act that paying people a lower wage simply because of their sex became illegal.[1] In the United States, the 1968 feminist protests against the Miss America pageant became a marker for the beginning of the movement. Those protesting the pageant argued that it reduced women to objects of beauty and that this status kept them in the home or in low paying jobs. This mode of protest was decidedly more shocking than the methods of first wave feminism. For example, to protest the pageant, women crowned a sheep as Miss America and threw objects such as bras and high heels into garbage cans. Second wave feminism targeted both legal rights, such as the right to an abortion and cultural expectations. The second wave is famous for such slogans as "the personal is political," which emphasized that the fight for equality had to happen within the home as much as outside the home. That is to say, the expectation that women would do all the cooking, cleaning, and caring for children is tied to the lack of opportunity for women in the public sphere. Second wave feminism worked to change both realms at once.

I will discuss third and fourth wave feminism in the following chapter, but for now I will point out that scholars contend that third wave feminism began in the 1990s as a response to the failures of second wave feminism (both its lack of racial and ethnic diversity and its more dogmatic expectations about how women should act once they have rebelled against patriarchy). Recently scholars have theorized that a fourth wave of feminism now exists, one addressing the failures of third wave feminism as well as defining itself through the internet.

A public discussion of the effects of ideology on women really began with second wave feminism, and feminist film theory arose out of this moment. While feminist film theorists have been involved in the debates over how we should define women, they have mostly been concerned with how women are represented in film and why. Film itself appeared in 1895, which means that feminism and the film industry have in part grown up together. Their relationship, however, has been somewhat fraught. Film as an art has reflected the biases of the social order and amplified the myths of woman as sexual object and woman as mother. Cinema has been an important vehicle for the dissemination of ideology surrounding women, and both feminism and feminist film theory have had recourse to the theory of ideology in order to critique society and film.

One might go so far as to contend that feminism and feminist film theory would be unthinkable without the theory of ideology. The theory of ideology helps feminists to theorize that the attributes associated with femininity emerge as a result of culture rather than nature. In what is probably the most famous feminist statement of all time, French philosopher Simone de Beauvoir argues: "One is not born, but rather becomes, woman."[2] Understanding how ideology works enables feminists to make sense of how half the population of the world could exist in a situation that oppresses them, just as it enables Marxism to comprehend how a majority of people on the planet would agree to work in order to enrich a small minority.

It is important then to begin with a discussion of ideology. Ideology as a concept was born out of the vibrant political debates of the French Revolution in the late 1700s. Specifically, French philosopher Antoine Louis Claude Destutt de Tracy coined the term to refer to a science of ideas.[3] He theorized that ideas arose from our bodily senses. For the time, this was a philosophy that flew in the face of religion and secular rule, causing Napoleon to ban the movement of philosophers interested in ideology in 1803.

Since then, the meaning of the term "ideology" has gone through several changes. Today, ideology refers to a system of beliefs. As much as political organizations and legal practices keep society functioning, no society can function without people believing in the ideas that support these practices. For example, the social order still very much relies on the family as the basic unit that structures daily life and produces new citizens to perpetuate it. As individuals, however, we believe in the idea of family as something essential to our own identity rather than just a structure that our social order needs and demands of us. Family itself is an idea that we invest ourselves in, whether we critique it or simply wholeheartedly celebrate it. Ideas about gender have been anchored in the belief in the family. In this sense, the idea of family is entwined with ideas about how women and men act. Family is ideological, and unpacking the ideology of the family has an important place in feminist theory.

One of the main aspects of ideology is that it hides itself. Even if ideology were to proclaim openly "this is ideology," such a statement would actually function as a form of concealment, hiding some other idea besides what the authorities openly articulated. Codes of behavior designed by a system of beliefs come to be thought of as expressions of nature rather than of culture. We see women, for example, as naturally more fit for nurturing and caring for children. The fact that this seems natural rather than cultural attests to the power of ideology. Despite its natural feel, this is a cultural idea since men can be just as nurturing. This idea of the nurturing woman is not just an idea; it has practical effects, which is why the social order constantly invokes it. The idea of the nurturing woman provides the basis for the exclusion of women from the work force, from politics, and from many other areas of social life. For centuries, patriarchal society proffered the idea that women had a biological disposition to nurturing and thus should stay in the domestic sphere.

One of the first tasks of ideology critique is to make people aware that entrenched codes of behavior are in fact cultural not biological. Oftentimes, just posing questions about entrenched beliefs provides enough distance from the beliefs so that people can see them as beliefs rather than simply as facts about the world. At its most basic, feminism has developed this questioning stance in relation to gender. Asking questions about the roles women are assigned to helps to contextualize those roles. For example, why would birthing a baby necessarily make a person better at raising that child? Why is it more appropriate for the woman to stay home with the children than for the man? Why do men and women take up certain kinds of roles within a family? Why can't there be different configurations of this? Why are men celebrated when they have many sexual partners while women are shunned? Why are female fashion trends so often restricting movement? This questioning begins to reveal that gender is an ideology, a system of beliefs in which we participate.

The term "ideology" prompts us to recognize that our individual beliefs are part of a larger system of beliefs. This does not mean that we don't have our own individual ideas. The concept of ideology suggests that our individual ideas always form in relation to the system of beliefs of the social order within which we live, even if in contradistinction to this system. Individual ideas that run counter to ideology can certainly be eventually taken up by an entire society. In this sense, ideology is always changing based on individual participation. Although ideology is always changing, it can also be incredibly recalcitrant. Individuals may work all their lives to change the prevailing ideology without having any success. Nevertheless, ideology can also change more quickly than we would expect.

We can see how radical change can happen if we consider something that seems absurd to us today, such as the sidesaddle. From a practical point of view, the sidesaddle makes no sense at all. It seems impossible to conceive of someone even having the idea for a device that forces women to put both legs on one side of a horse while riding it rather that placing one leg on each side. But this shows the lengths to which patriarchal ideology drives people to think. Since the 1300s until the mid-twentieth century women rode sidesaddle because society considered it unladylike to ride astride. In 2015, not sixty years since the tradition completely died, it seems laughable that a woman would be denied riding astride a horse. But during the reign of the sidesaddle, society shunned women who defied the tradition.

Society considered women who didn't ride sidesaddle to be unruly, unfeminine, and overly sexual. The sidesaddle restricted women's movement, which is a common aspect of women's fashion. It also prevented women from being in complete control of their horse, and many riders and their horses were injured due to this strange one-sided configuration. There had been individual women in history who eschewed the tradition, most famously Catherine the Great, but the force of their individual personalities was not enough to change the recalcitrant ideology that proclaimed riding astride to be unfeminine.[4] How did such an entrenched social expectation change so completely and quickly? The change did not happen in one instant, but once transcended, the past tradition seemed impossible. That is to say, we could not imagine going back to it. The sidesaddle is a good example because it is an item created specifically to embody an idea of femininity that then restricted and controlled women's bodies. It's easier to see in hindsight how the sidesaddle was an *idea* of femininity because it is a material object that human beings produced on the basis of a way of thinking. It reinforced society's belief system that women needed to be protected, controlled, and restricted in order to be women. The sidesaddle is a material object that represented the ideology of femininity at that time. It's less easy to see the way we ourselves participate in ideology, especially when it involves our own bodies. How we sit, groom ourselves, and dress—all reflect our relation to the prevailing ideology.

Ideology as a concept is somewhat simple, yet it can shed voluminous light on the complex workings of how individuals relate to their social orders. Belief systems govern our behavior and our social laws. Sometimes laws in place no longer reflect prevailing ideologies and must be changed, and sometimes the creation of new laws helps to create new ideologies. Ideology is not the law itself but a way of relating to the law. Law is constraining and uncomfortable, which is why all people become nervous when the police begin to follow them. Ideology, however, gives us a feeling of comfort in our relationship to the law. It provides us a position in which the force of the law seems muted and even friendly.

The concept of ideology allows us to understand the constructed, dynamic, powerful nature of ideas, of the very ideas within which we live and think. When we use the phrase "to think outside the box," it usually means to try to think outside of the prevailing system of ideas. Ironically, this has now become a very ideological way of thinking—major corporations encourage their employees "to think outside the box" and advertisements call for consumers to do so—which shows that ideology has the ability to bring every oppositional position within its functioning. But in some sense, the challenge of thinking outside the box remains because this is the essence of ideology critique, and it becomes even more imperative when ideology itself seems to demand this.

For feminists, the concept of ideology allowed them to theorize why women were in certain roles and how we might change these ideas. Feminism analyzed the expectations of women that seemed natural in order to reveal their constructedness. Feminism developed as a questioning stance in relation to the ideologies of gender as they worked to defamiliarize seemingly natural assumptions. As long as feminism exists, the critique of ideology will be central to its project.

In some ways, Destutt de Tracy's theory that ideas arose from our bodily senses, while now completely outdated, was a critique of ideology. His empiricism was a reaction against the dominance of ideas, a way of conceiving the genesis of ideas rather than just accepting their dominance. Much of the way we interact with our own belief system is not to think about it but to simply enact it. We assess people and situations in an instant based on our ideas but in such a way that feels more like a bodily reaction than a cerebral exercise.

After Destutt de Tracy's initial theory of ideology, Karl Marx's analysis of capital marks the next crucial point in the history of ideology critique. Cowritten in 1845 with Frederick Engels, *The German Ideology* argued that belief systems had the status of a camera obscura that inverts the image. Specifically, Marx and Engels argued that people were blind to the way economic systems shaped us. *The German Ideology* critiques ideology for disguising the material basis of society and convincing us that ideas rule the world. For Marx, ideology was a belief that ideas shaped the world not material influences. Once people saw, Marx theorized, the material causes of society, then they would no longer be duped by the notion that ideas shaped the world and would thus be free to break the chains of oppression.

Later, Louis Althusser's essay "Ideology and Ideological State Apparatuses" pushed the definition of ideology further. Like Marx, Althusser believed in the oppressive nature of ideology, but unlike Marx, he did not think that one could simply get out of it. He detailed all the ways in which institutions such as schools, churches, medical establishments, and the family propagated ideology. He believed ideology hailed the individual in order to force the individual to think of itself as a subject free to act as it wants in the world. Althusser called this process "interpellation," and he saw it exemplified in the action of a police officer who yells "Hey you" at an individual. When the individual recognizes itself as the subject of this hail, ideology interpellates the individual.

The lasting impact of Althusser's theory is the conviction, still widely held today, that there is no outside to ideology. We can't just erase ideology and live in an ideology-free zone. This means that we have to work within ideology to change it rather than just concentrate on tearing it down or attempting to inhabit a utopian outside space.

Other theorists working in psychoanalytic traditions suggested that a theory of ideology should acknowledge that ideology is both conscious and unconscious. People can act on their beliefs without consciously thinking about ideology. We do this all the time: in the ways that we treat each other, in the things that we desire, in the goals that we strive for, and so on. In this sense, our unconscious reactions are especially embedded in ideology. The more we behave socially without thinking about it, the more invested we are in ideology. This is why theorists and activists alike work hard to defamiliarize everyday habits, hoping that if people can step outside their natural responses then they might see that these responses are in fact constructed and can be changed.

Ideology necessarily functions by hiding its own constructed nature. People don't think, for example, that they are part of a family because it is the prevailing social structure and though constructed it is better than being alone and hungry. They believe that they love their parents, that they simply want to eventually have a family of their own, and that they believe in romantic love as the base of the family. In this way, one of the key aspects of ideology is that individuals assume that they believe in the family because it feels right, not because it is the prevailing system of ideas. This unthinking relation to these ideas is part of why ideology is so powerful. Seeing the contradictory nature of ideology can throw ideology into view and turn an individual's relationship to it into a much more critical and conscious relationship. Women often have this experience when they know they are capable of working in an appealing job, but they are told that their place is in the home, or they must ride with a sidesaddle, or that they can't direct a big budget Hollywood film. Feminism arose from women experiencing these contradictions that ideology could not fully obscure.

Ideology does, however, work to erase the appearance of these contradictions that throw the constructed nature of ideology into relief. As thinking individuals, we have the capacity to live with great contradiction, but when that contradiction is made fully evident, it is difficult to continue believing in the two contradictory ideas. For example, today we have an idea of equality on the one hand and yet some accept the idea that women have less natural aptitude for mathematics and science—and thus make up just a small percentage working in these fields. Even though feminists decry this inequality, it nonetheless is accepted as an active ideology. This position has enough traction that even the president of Harvard can feel free to espouse it in public.[5]

One of the main contradictions within ideology that feminism works to point out and tear down is the contradictory ideals of femininity. Feminism has long worked to combat the prevailing ideologies about women. But the ideologies about women are particularly tricky because of their contradictory nature and the multiple ways we work to ignore these contradictions. Throughout much of modern western society, the ideal of femininity has been completely split between the woman as sexual and the woman as nurturing, between the prostitute and the mother. Rather than imagining being sexual and being nurturing as just some possible aspects of women (among others, including smart, aggressive, violent, funny, innovative, mean, loving, and so on), these two qualities become definitive and exaggerated. They become the basis for fantasmatic dueling myths of femininity that have had a huge impact on the social expectations of women. The wager of feminism is that recognizing the ridiculous nature of this contradiction might have the effect of tearing down both sides of the contradiction so that they can be replaced with a recognition of the fundamental problem of subjectivity itself.

One of the conundrums of these contradictory expectations of femininity is that if one inhabits one of them, then one lacks in the other. Both of these myths of femininity have their social benefits: if a woman is sexual, then men desire her, and if a woman is a mother, then she has power over the domestic sphere. The two positions bar women from the public sphere and from opportunities in the workplace. That is to say, if a woman is overly sexual, no one in the workplace takes her seriously, and if a woman devotes herself to mothering, she will not have time to work or receive serious consideration from colleagues. This contradiction birthed feminism. It reacted to the impossible nature of these expectations and the real world limitations that these myths put on women's lives.

Film as a nascent industry was wide open to women filmmakers, but by the 1930s, when the industry solidified in Los Angeles, it became completely closed to them. It remains relatively closed to women today. In 2015, in fact, the ACLU brought a case against Hollywood to address the blatant sexism of the industry's hiring practices in relation to women. Film became the dominant medium of visual art and communication in the twentieth century, and it remains a significant presence in the twenty-first century. As a result, representations of gender in film, television, and other media, around the globe have a profound impact on cultural expectations of gender. From Hollywood film to independent film, from advertising to Internet pornography, from you tube videos to smart phone apps, the contradictory images of women are more present now than ever before.

Feminist film theory draws on both film theory and feminist theory to analyze the impact of these representations. It also often turns to female directed films for alternative possibilities. This book will focus on some of the main ways feminist film theorists have approached representations of women and their discoveries. I will focus specifically on three of the main ways that feminist film theorists have approached these issues: theories of identification, theories about how the camera frames the female body and why, and analyses of the female auteur. Theories of identification, and the plethora of critiques lodged against these theories, provided a way for feminist film theorists to analyze how the film form—the camera work, editing, and narrative structure—reinforced the contradictory myths of femininity. Eventually, feminist film theorists moved away from the concept of identification toward concepts such as engagement, which emphasizes desire and multiple ways of interacting with a film. Theories about how the camera frames the female body also considered how the film form produced ideas of femininity but specifically looked at how the camera presents the woman's body. Along with this, feminist film theory investigated the impact of the way the camera framed only certain types of female bodies and character types that stemmed from the original contradiction between the prostitute and the mother, including the myriad types of working women that are still overly sexualized and the types of mothers that are represented. Feminist film theorists have also looked to the female filmmaker to see how alternatives to these images can be created. In the following chapter, I will go into these three approaches in depth, giving examples that will lead to the analysis of Agnés Varda's *Cléo from 5 to 7* as an exemplary text for the exploration of feminist film theory.

Notes

1   Today there is still a pay gap, with a woman making 78 cents for each dollar that men make. This number is just a symbol, since race and class also play a large role in the pay gap, so that certain women earn more than others. In addition, some states and professions are better than others, but across the board, it is still true that women earn less than men. Hollywood is actually one of the industries in which the pay gap is very significant: the top paid actors make 2.5 times more than the top paid actresses.

2   Simone de Beauvoir, *The Second Sex*, trans. Constance Borde and Sheila Malovany-Chevallier (New York: Alfred A. Knopf, 2010), 283.

3   His first book on ideology came out in 1801. See Antoine Louis Claude Destutt de Tracy, *Éléments D'idéologie* (Paris: Vrin, 1970).

4   There were cultures that never adapted the sidesaddle, such as Hawaii and Iceland.

5   In January 2005, Lawrence Summers, then President of Harvard University, contended that fewer woman had jobs in science and engineering at universities because, in addition to social factors, they had less natural aptitude for the kind of thinking that these positions require.

CHAPTER ONE

Feminist Film Theory

Feminism and identification

There is, of course, neither one type of feminism nor one type of feminist film theory. Most major ideas within feminist film theory inspire various competing positions. Nonetheless, it is this very struggle among feminist film theorists to analyze how cinema interacts with gender that constitutes its vibrancy and urgency. The contradictory ideals of femininity (sex object on the one hand versus mother on the other) inform the vast majority of representations of women throughout the history of film. Feminist film theory works to highlight this contradiction as well as debate its effects. Identification, framing the woman's body, and the importance of the female auteur are three concepts that have been lightning rods for debate within feminist film theory. Additionally, these three concepts mark the concern in feminist film theory with how the female body has been employed to sell ideology. Feminist film theorists often look to the female filmmakers who similarly grapple with this question and can provide new insight into it.

In *Cléo from 5 to 7*, as I'll demonstrate in the following chapter, Agnès Varda—by privileging spectator engagement over spectator identification and through her unique framing of the woman's body—reveals the contradictions at the heart of ideal femininity. Namely, she reveals that the image of ideal femininity both creates identity and erases it at the same time.

Depicting this conflict prompts spectators to become aware of the disjunction at the core of femininity; it also prompts them to analyze the relationship between being a woman, ideological ideal female beauty, and identity as such. In this way, Varda engages ideal beauty while making the viewer aware of its relationship to nothingness—the fact that there is nothing substantial to it. The following investigations into identification, framing the woman's body, and the importance of the female auteur identify separate concepts in feminist film theory but also come together to illuminate new modes of feminist thinking.

Feminist film theorists, especially from the 1970s and 1980s, argued that identification—created through camera positioning, editing, and narrative structure—solidified the dominance of the male position. They argued that spectators identified with the male character and that filmmakers built the entire structure of the film around this initial identification. Others, including black feminists, queer feminists, and third wave feminists argued that film's address to its spectator was much more contradictory, flexible, and multilayered than early feminists had suggested. These critiques revealed the importance of theorizing identity as such, urging it to be both more universal and at the same time more aware of the intersections between the universal and the particular. The ideological contradictions within femininity had particular expressions but also resonated because of their relationship with universal ideas about identity. Feminism takes as its primary task the investigation of these relationships between the particular and the universal of female identity. In this light, the questions of where spectators entered the text, how this occurred, and what effect it had on spectators were essential questions for how film interacts with ideology.

Identification began as a fundamental concept in film theory in general. For this reason, it functions as an umbrella term for several issues, but theories of identification tend to consider the way in which the spectator identifies with the main character. Theories about identification also address how the spectator invests in the filmic process in general. These theories pose such questions as: what is the relationship between the spectator and their enjoyment of the film? Is identification the vehicle for the enjoyment of the spectator and her investment in the trajectory of the film? Feminist film theory intervened in this discussion by arguing that identification was a politically charged process that reinforced gender stereotypes, sustained hierarchies, and in general contributed to the oppression of women. This argument, which will be explained at length here, had a significant impact on film studies itself. It also began a debate, which continues to this day, about how feminist film theory should be defined and whether the very concept of identification is useful for feminist film theory.

There are several key theoretical developments that occur in the twenty years leading up to the moment when feminist film theorists, beginning in the 1970s and 1980s, argued that identification—manipulated through camera positioning, editing, and narrative structure—solidified the dominance of the male position in the social order. One of the key developments were the ideas of French film theorists Christian Metz and Jean-Louis Baudry, who originated what is now known as screen theory.

Screen theory

Published in 1970 in the journal *Cinéthique*, Jean-Louis Baudry's "Ideological Effects of the Basic Cinematographic Apparatus" combines the ideas of several prominent theorists to explain the power of cinema. For Baudry, the cinema screen acts as a mirror reflecting not reality but a fantasy of reality back to us. This fantasy is ideology itself. That is, it is the cultural belief system we are steeped in which then reinforces itself. This idea is a combination of both psychoanalyst Jacques Lacan's essay on the mirror stage and Marxist philosopher Louis Althusser's conception of ideology.[1] Lacan theorizes that the mirror stage in a child's development occurs when she looks into the mirror and identifies with an illusion of bodily control rather than recognizing her actual stage of development. Key to this idea is that it is the initial misrecognition that prompts the development of the ego and the sense of wholeness that accompanies it. Althusser, on the other hand, conceives how concrete individuals became enmeshed in ideology by relating to themselves as subjects. He believes that ideology hails individuals who have no choice but to accept the hail. Even in the act of rejecting the hail, one misrecognizes oneself as its addressee. The source of the power of ideology, for Althusser, is that even under the thrall of ideology individuals still mistakenly feel that they have freedom. Althusser feels that this mistaken idea gave ideology its overriding power to dominate the individual.[2]

Baudry brings these ideas to bear on two aspects of the cinema: that we are aligned with the camera to feel a sense of mastery over the image and that narrative editing styles work to hide the constructed nature of the film. According to Baudry, this makes cinema a tool of ideology. Baudry argues, "It is an apparatus destined to obtain a precise ideology effect, necessary to the dominant ideology: creating a fantasmatization of the subject, it collaborates with a marked efficacity in the maintenance of idealism."[3] Ideology, according to Baudry, was implicitly harmful because it molded individuals according to its dictates and all the while made them feel as though it was their choice. At the time, Baudry's conception of how cinema operates was an essential tool for seeing the way ideology functioned, but later its limitations became evident. Nonetheless, this critique was a powerful tool for feminist theorists to explain how culture reinforces women's oppression.

Christian Metz also had an impact on feminist film theory by providing detailed tools to analyze a film. His project was to understand why film had such a significant impact on the spectator's imagination. Metz was less interested in ideology than in the film's structure, including the camera techniques, editing, and story. Metz was, like many in France at the time, interested in structuralism, specifically in relation to linguistics and psychoanalysis.

Metz views the film as the site of an imaginary relationship for the spectator that hides the structure informing that relationship. As a result, he understands the project of the film theorist to be one of making the structure evident. The theorist explains what the film obscures through its emphasis on image. One makes clear to spectators that a film is not just a story without a teller (as it first appears) but a discourse articulated from a specific (tendentious) perspective.

Both Metz and Baudry theorized that the film's structure affected the spectator's psyche. They analyzed film as a system of signifiers that interacted with the spectator's imagination in powerful ways and reinforced social structures. Their approach provided important tools for feminists to begin to make strong arguments about how this system of signifiers defined gender. These were powerful analytic tools that brought culture to the fore, but Metz and Baudry did not talk about gender. Nor did they proffer a theory about how representation or the lack of representation had material consequences on people in society.

Other influences on 1970s feminism: From Beauvoir to the Civil Rights Movement

Feminist film theorists of the 1970s began to address the lack of gender awareness in Screen theory. But this project did not emerge out of thin air. It had its roots in the feminist movement, which was a powerful force in western society throughout the twentieth century and especially in the 1960s and 1970s. The feminist movement took its bearing from practical responses to oppression, but it also relied on the insights of feminist theory.

There were several prominent feminist theorists whose ideas opened up the possibility for feminist film theory. Through the lens of existentialism, French theorist Simone de Beauvoir's *The Second Sex* (1949) was instrumental in laying out a structural analysis of how women take on their identity. Beauvoir famously argues that women are not born women but rather they become women. In *The Second Sex*, she sketches out women's relation to economics, religion, marriage, biology, and their own psyche. She argues that men constitute the center of the social and that women have the status of the other. Beauvoir argues, "History has shown us that men have always held all the concrete powers; from patriarchy's earliest times they have deemed it useful to keep woman in a state of dependence; their codes were set up against her; and she was thus concretely established as the Other."[4] Reproduction does not require that society constructs women in this way, but our specific social order under patriarchy perpetuates it. Beauvoir reveals that society as a whole relies on the idea that man is the subject and woman is his complementary other. This other is his prize, his inspiration, and, at the same time, what he fears. Woman is bound to the man, and her otherness defines his subjectivity. In this sense, according to Beauvoir, women are integral to society and yet necessarily inferior.

For Beauvoir, this social order is inextricably bound up with the imagery of women, which illustrates for women what they are supposed to be modeling themselves on. It is in this sense that she points the way for future feminist film theory. The images of women are powerful and instructive, but they are also confusing. The common images for women, she finds, take two opposed forms—the mother and the sexual object. Women do not have one ideal but rather have a pair of contradictory ideals. One might contend that the princess is a key stepping stone to becoming a wife and then a mother, but the qualities, Beauvoir points out, do not necessarily translate insofar as one lends itself to the other. These representations, therefore, can never be fully realized since by embodying one ideal you necessarily fail in the other.

In response to this oppressive situation, Beauvoir calls for people to recognize each other as subjects and thus for an end to woman's position as man's other. Along the same lines, she demands political and economic equality for women. Beauvoir's ideas are considered the early start to the second wave since they tied the psyche to culture and to economics, which is what the second wave emphasized. While Beauvoir certainly revealed how men played a role in women's oppression, she also analyzed why women bought into the system as well as how they contributed to it.

US theorist Betty Friedan's treatise on the situation of women in *The Feminine Mystique* (1963) played a similarly important role in feminism's second wave, though her involvement was much more direct. In addition to writing her polemical text, Friedan cofounded the National Organization of Women in the United States in 1966. Friedan's book attacked the ideals of femininity and womanhood from the 1950s. She felt that women were sliding backwards from the rights they had secured with the first wave of feminism and the passage of 19th Amendment to the US Constitution for women's suffrage in 1920. While women, for example, were going to college in the 1950s, they often saw it as place to find a husband rather than a place to develop their minds. Along with these statistics, Freidan reports in her book that girls were expected to assume sexual looks earlier and earlier. The expectation of younger sexual expression directly contradicted with the expectations of motherhood. While her critique was impactful, many critiqued Friedan for concentrating solely on upper-class white women. The picture Friedan painted may have been true for white upper-class women, but it certainly wasn't true for lower-class black and white women, who had been working outside the home their whole lives to support their families. Nonetheless, the prevailing fantasies of femininity during the 1950s, Friedan argues, affected the social order in general and needed to be changed. Her book was as much an exposé as a call to action. It argued that the social order's image of femininity, perpetuated by the media, was a major contributor to this feminine mystique that was keeping women away from finding careers or working outside of the home at all. This led to many women who were entirely dissatisfied with their lives but didn't understand why.

From the standpoint of feminist theory, Beauvoir's concept that the social order constructs women and Friedan's argument that cultural expectations blinded women allowed for women in the 1970s to begin to theorize their position in society with more sophistication. It also allowed them to imagine how changes to cultural expectations could begin. While first wave feminism fought for rights to vote and attend college, second wave feminism saw the need for culture to change. Identification with cultural expectations and media depictions of femininity became one of the battlegrounds of feminism. Women, according to second wave feminism, identified with expectations that restricted their behavior. Both Beauvoir and Friedan, through vastly different approaches, opened people's eyes to these nuances of culture. Beauvoir linked this to philosophical questions about existence, while Friedan provided more practical observations—both of which allowed feminists to see their situation in a new way and begin their own analyses.

Another important social, theoretical, and political movement that influenced feminist film theory as well as feminism in the United States was the Civil Rights movement. The Civil Rights movement argued that oppression and representation—in government, laws, popular culture— operated together. The movement made clear that without equal representation African Americans could never have equality in the United States. The Civil Rights movements worked on many fronts, including laws about voting, segregation of public spaces, equal housing, and equal work. As the Civil Rights movement worked on each of these issues, the question of equality within cultural representations also became a pressing issue. Civil Rights workers realized that representation in history, in art, in museums, on television, and in film had a significant impact on swaying public opinion.

Women working for the civil rights movement brought these approaches to the feminist movement. In this way, the Civil Rights movement and the feminist movement in the 1970s worked together on the contradictions of identification as well as their effects on the social order. This convergence of theories about the power of cultural expectations reveals the entwined nature of theorizing gender and race. In subsequent decades, sexuality and class were also a key part of this discussion, so that in contemporary theory the problem of identity becomes even more complex. Nevertheless, this does not mitigate the importance of individual theories. It is the particular revelations of, for example, critical race studies, feminist theory, or queer theory that allows for a thorough investigation of the universal questions of identity and the universal questions then shed light on the particular theories.

Additionally, while each of these approaches had been accused at different times of ignoring the concerns of the others, the contemporary theorist can see the concerns in common, and can approach a topic—say, a film or a television show— with an eye toward the contradictions of identity that reside therein. From this point of contradiction, one can interrogate identity. Feminist film theory today can hold onto the concerns that have to do with the representations of gender through its awareness of the inherently contradictory nature of identity. This approach will lead to a more complex analysis that illuminates identity's relation to the social order. For example, how did race, sexuality, or class play into the spectator's cultural expectations of gender? The idea here is not moving toward endless specificity but rather toward a theoretical approach that grasps the relation between the particular and the universal contradictions of identity. Grasping more completely the intersectional nature of identity allows one to see how ideology works to obscure the contradictions of identity.

Feminist film theory emerged out of a combination of screen theory, the Civil Rights movement's emphasis on equal representation in cultural spaces, and early second wave feminists' critique of inequality between the sexes. Feminist film theorists such as Laura Mulvey and Claire Johnston laid the foundations for the debates that were to unfold in feminist film theory over the next several decades. They investigated such topics as: what type of female characters appeared in mainstream films; how did the spectator relate to male and female characters; what was the relationship between the sexes in the film; and how did this relate to the current cultural expectations of gender, race, and sexuality. They also considered how all of these issues influenced the lack of equality between men and women in the social order. These early feminist film theorists had many disagreements, which I will lay out, but they all in some way or another considered how the politics of gender representation in film interacted with cultural expectations. They analyzed how women were represented in the narrative, in the mise-en-scène, and through the editing. Additionally, they often theorized how filmmakers could change their approach thereby affecting the social order.

The advent of feminist film theory

British film theorist Laura Mulvey's most significant contribution to feminist film theory was her emphasis on the way film form engaged in the cultural expectations of gender. She argued her point in her essay "Visual Pleasure and Narrative Cinema," which was published in the British journal *Screen* in 1975.[5] While the argument about gender and film form was utterly unique, many aspects of the essay were consistent with the work of other writers for *Screen*. Thus, eventually film studies came to think of the work at this time in *Screen* along with the ideas of Christian Metz and Jean-Louis Baudry as Screen theory.[6] Screen theory focuses on how the spectator identifies with the film itself. Generally, Screen theory contends that the structure of a film provides a sense of mastery to the spectator so that she can ignore the constructed nature of the film and instead experience the film as a dream world that she inhabits. The set-up of the dark theater, the editing that worked to hide itself, and the linear narrative structure creates a situation in which the spectator helplessly absorbs the ideology that Hollywood film proffers. Screen theory views identification as the way the spectator experiences pleasure in the film and the primary way that cinema transmits ideology.

There were several theorists at *Screen* who brought gender to bear on this discussion. Besides Laura Mulvey, feminist theorists Claire Johnston and Pam Cook wrote pathbreaking essays that refigured how one interpreted gender on film. For example, in her essay "Women's Cinema as Counter-Cinema" (1973), Johnston argues that images of women in film do not resemble actual women's lives.[7] Instead, each character represents a patriarchal fantasy about women. In her analysis of John Ford's Westerns, she illustrates how the female characters represent home or civilization rather than being protagonists in their own right. In this way, she argues, women become symbols of cultural beliefs rather than active participants in their own society. When spectators watch these films, the representations create a politics of gender that denies women agency through these repeated tropes. Male characters are also often symbols as well, but they do not have such a limited range of representation.

Laura Mulvey's "Visual Pleasure and Narrative Cinema" addresses a different area as she maps out exactly how men and women are positioned within the narrative and in relation to the spectator. Mulvey argues that in classical Hollywood cinema the male character is most often the protagonist. Mulvey explains that this means his character's desires move the narrative along. Visually, this manifests itself in multiple ways. The male character is often presented striding through the environment, and directors tend to film the entire male body as he moves through the frame. Furthermore, it is the male point of view that dominates the film. That is to say, we experience the world visually from his point of view often seeing an eye line match of what he is looking at. The spectator is aligned with him as the protagonist and visually through these eye line match shots, which Mulvey calls the male gaze.

The important counterpart to this male character is the female lead, who is not the protagonist though she is often whom the male character desires. Or she is the mystery that the male character has to figure out. In this way, she is the object that complements him as subject. Mulvey argues that the film presents her status as object of male desire visually. The female character, she explains, does not appear striding through the frame as she moves the narrative along. Instead, the film shows her contained within the filmic space waiting for a male character to see her. Hollywood films often combine this with a particular way of filming the female body. Specifically, directors shoot the female body in pieces through close-ups of the legs, breasts, and other body parts. This inscribes them solely as a sexual object. Their representation signals the male's desire rather than their own, and mainstream cinema rarely addresses female desire at all. Additionally, it seldom displays the female character's point of view. In other words, the spectator has no opportunity to align herself with the perspective of the female character. Though we enjoy looking at her, we do not identify with her.

Mulvey sees the woman in Hollywood cinema as the bearer of meaning rather than the maker of meaning. In Mulvey's terms, the woman's "to-be-looked-at-ness" generates her status as object and bearer of meaning. Her appearance and sexual allure indicates her status as an object for the spectator. Mulvey argues, "Mainstream film coded the erotic into the language of the dominant patriarchal order."[8] In this way, film form, according to Mulvey, projects a male fantasy onto the female figure. The woman is more aligned with spectacle than narrative and even at times stops the flow of the narrative. The spectator identifies with the male character and sees the female character as an object, as a prize, as a fantasy but never as a subject.

The impact of Mulvey's essay was tremendous, and it became the most anthologized essays in film studies. It also began a lengthy debate in feminist film theory about how spectators identify with and find pleasure in a film, as well as what impact this has on equality in the social order. Mulvey advocated critiquing pleasure, specifically the pleasure the spectator received from the above technical practices. She argued for tearing down cinematic pleasure in order to end male dominated cinema and thereby confront inequality. In the 1970s, Mulvey and Johnston believed that cinema could effect social change. They did not, however, believe that this change could happen within a mainstream film form, which they argued was part of the problem. On the one hand, this stance helped to encourage the exciting growth of an independent feminist filmmaking movement. On the other hand, it cut off mainstream media as a potential site of political engagement and thus lost adherents when feminists began to embrace popular culture as an important site for political contestation.

Black feminist film theory

Some of the first serious critiques of these early essays pointed out that they also focus solely on representations of white women. The film examples that Mulvey chooses do not involve the depiction of black women or other women of color. As a result of this omission, Mulvey and the other early feminist film theorists tend to miss precisely how identity functions, especially the intersectional nature of identity. In other words, individuals are not just men or women, but they also are defined by their race, ethnicity, sexuality, class, and so on. While it might be difficult to discuss all these identities at once, ignoring all but one creates a restricted theory.

Theorizing the intersectional nature of identity inevitably points to the paradox of identity as such and allows the theorist to acknowledge the relationship of the individual to the larger social order. The paradox of identity is that it both exists and doesn't exist. It can be inhabited and it is impossible to inhabit at the same time. It is what limits and restricts you while at the same time it makes thought and creativity possible because it embroils you in the social order. Identity is as paradoxical as language, which has infinite possibility and yet rigidly confines one's thought at the same time.

Early feminist film theory excluded race from their ideas in several ways. On the one hand, the essays focus only on white characters. On the other hand, they don't theorize this whiteness in any way. Early feminist film theorists thus cut off a potential investigation into the paradoxes of femininity and identity. This mirrored similar exclusions happening within feminist theory and activism. Black feminist theorists in the 1980s pointed out the second wave's erasure of black women and the lack of complex thinking in regards to identity and femininity.[9]

Kimberle Crenshaw's "Mapping the Margins: Intersectionality, Identity Politics and Violence against Women of Color" (1991) had a major impact on feminist theory as well as critical race theory.[10] As a lawyer and law professor, Crenshaw came at the question of identity politics from the point of view of the justice system. She was well acquainted with the material consequences of sexism and racism through legal decisions. Additionally, she had an intimate knowledge of how the larger system of law defined people in ways that were consistent with mainstream ideas of gender and race but which had devastating consequences for them as citizens. Through the details of real cases involving violence against women of color, Crenshaw lays out the inadequacies of seeing feminism and civil rights as completely separate.

She explains that cases would come through in which the court would accept a gender-centered case or a race-centered case. They would listen to the way a black woman was discriminated against because of her gender or because of her race but never the two together. Crenshaw develops her theory of intersectionality in relation to these experiences. She argues that the law needs to acknowledge the intersectional nature of identity and contends that it is unjust if it does not. Her theory of intersectionality has gained traction among many feminists as a more complex way to understand how gender operates in society.

Although bell hooks did not take up this term, her essay "The Oppositional Gaze: Black Female Spectators" also pointed out the lack of intersectional thinking in feminist film theory. More specifically, hooks addresses feminist film theory and challenges Mulvey's notion of identification as the only mode of engaging with a film; hooks also theorizes the potential of an oppositional gaze or look. She points out that when the United States denied black people's rights, the oppression often included dictums that black people should not look at white people. This was a powerful form of racism and points to the power of the look. In response, hooks claims, black people cultivated an oppositional gaze to enact and symbolize rebellion. As hooks explains: "The 'gaze' has been and is a site of resistance for colonized black people globally."[11] For hooks, the oppositional gaze is the key for interrogating the gaze of the oppressive social authority.

With regard to films and television, she argues, black audiences have an awareness of the way that visual pleasure functions. They know that a fantasy of whiteness perpetuated through racist stereotypes dominates mainstream cinema and television. This awareness leads to a different way of engaging film and television—an oppositional engagement built on critical awareness. Black spectators use this oppositional gaze in order to constitute themselves as resisting spectators. Viewing mainstream films with a critical awareness of their patriarchal white emphasis can transform even popular cinema into a site for rebellion. Like many feminist film theorists, hooks also calls for us to look to black female filmmakers who can pose alternative narratives and visual structures that allow us to engage in filmic depictions of the United States in a new way.

Black feminist theory's critique of second wave feminism and its erasure of blackness was also, as bell hooks makes evident, a critique of the theory of identification. Second wave feminists looked to identification as a theoretical concept that explained the dominance of patriarchy in films. This approach argued that films—through their camera work, editing, and narrative structure—built a world in which women were objects and men were subjects. Male subjects had the power of the look, and the spectators bought into this social structure by identifying with the main male character. For these theorists, our enjoyment of films derives from our sense of mastery in the film, and this comes about through a process of identification.

Black feminist theory, however, challenged the idea that the only way a spectator entered the film was through identification. Excluded by the interplay of looks and the lack of black representation, black women, hooks argues, were not addressed by this mainstream mode of identification. She points out, however, that one way black female spectators found pleasure in these texts is through an oppositional gaze that they employed to engage the film. Moreover, hooks suggests that this oppositional gaze is not necessary when watching films that do not present a white patriarchal worldview. Importantly, the film with a non-white patriarchal worldview does not rely on identification as it instead generates multiple ways of engaging the viewer. Kimberle Crenshaw's theory of intersectionality similarly ruptures the idea of identification as a worthwhile feminist tool. Identification as an effective theoretical tool for feminism thus began to crumble by the 1990s.[12]

From identification to engagement

The critique of identification that black feminists advanced met with other champions. Queer theorists also discussed identifying with classical films in alternative ways, thus throwing early feminist film theory claims about identification again into question. Queer theory brought the question of pleasure and desire back into the equation. Rather than being part of the ideological problem that, for example, Mulvey saw it to be, pleasure and desire for queer theorists actually motivated an alternative looking strategy that undercut even the patriarchal form of classical Hollywood.

Patricia White's *Uninvited*, for example, lays out an investigation into the lesbian spectator's relationship to classical Hollywood film. She argues, contra Mulvey, that there are different positions one can take up relative to the film's structure. White's book came out in 1999 and evinces a debt to black feminist theory. She explicitly claims that the book "is influenced by the theorizing of race, representation, and strategies of oppositional viewing, and these feminist studies have in turn influenced lesbian and gay studies."[13] Whereas Mulvey analyzed the male gaze, White contends that lesbians don't desire the male gaze; instead, they take up unexpected spaces and points of view offered in a film. This rebellion against the structure does not happen as an active political gesture but instead happens because of pleasure and desire. Pleasure is the very feeling that Mulvey sought to destroy because she felt it was formed by patriarchal structures. White, however, reveals that desire can also be the point of resistance rather than be the conduit for ideology.

Theories of identification arose out of an attempt to bring psychoanalysis to bear on the cinema, but recent psychoanalytic media theorists have also challenged these early theories as misinterpretations of psychoanalysis. The impetus for this challenge to Screen theory was a return to Jacques Lacan's actual thought as articulated in his seminars, none of which were available when Screen theory first emerged. When looking over Lacan's entire corpus, it became clear that the mirror stage—the foundation of the theory of identification that Mulvey and others develop—was not such a key aspect of his thought. Concepts like enjoyment (or *jouissance*), desire, alienation, and the relation to the object dominate Lacan's seminars, and in his seminar devoted to identification, he never discusses it in the way that Screen theory does. Lacan's focus is not on ideological interpellation but on the split nature of our subjectivity and how enjoyment and desire relate to this splitting.

Psychoanalytic feminist film theorist Joan Copjec originated the critique of Screen theory and Laura Mulvey's version of feminist film theory.[14] Though other feminists attacked Mulvey on feminist grounds, Copjec focused on Mulvey's misreading of psychoanalysis. She proposes that Screen theory erred in its conception of the spectator's relationship to the screen. Spectators relate to the film through desire rather than through a sense of mastery. Desire, for psychoanalysis, is not a simple process of wanting something and going after it. Desire has its basis in loss, but rather than aiming to eradicate loss with a fullness, it aims at perpetuating lack. Our desire is necessarily unconscious because it constantly undermines our self-interest, and it deprives us of mastery over the world. Encountering points that motivate our desire can keep us engaged in the film, but this engagement does not give us a sense of mastery. In *Read My Desire*, Copjec argues that encountering objects of our desire can create a lack of mastery as we realize our own complicity in the structures of the narrative and the society. In other words, investment in the cinematic experience stems more from failure than from the pleasure of mastery.

Here, Copjec inverts Screen theory's conception of how film functions ideologically. Rather than being seduced by an idea of mastery—through identification with the male protagonist—over the world, Copjec theorizes that the spectator is instead drawn to intersections of the endless symbolic fictions that are woven through a film. The narrative structure, visual style, composition, and editing choices work together to engage the spectator's desire. At moments throughout a film, these complicated structures coalesce in an object, a trope of editing, or a narrative turn—to name a few examples—that both engages our desire and reveals our own unconscious investment in the events depicted on the screen. This may be pleasurable, traumatic, or anxiety producing, but it rivets our psyche and invests us in the film. We see ourselves as complicit in the structures of the film at the intersections of the symbolic fictions, intersections that often expose these fictions as much as they may shore them up.

While arguably more complicated, Copjec's revision opens a much more flexible and nuanced way to analyze the undeniable draw of the moving image and its role in society. Of her book, Copjec says: "If this book may be said to have one intention, it is this: to urge analysts of culture to become literate in desire, to learn how to read what is inarticulable in cultural statements."[15] Her approach also works well with, if not demands, an intersectional approach to identity. It considers the spectator's relationship with the film not as identification with one character but rather as an engagement of desire, which can be an experience that is conscious or unconscious, pleasurable or painful, and can happen at expected or unexpected intersections. These intersections reveal both identity's particular variations and its universal paradoxes. In light of Copjec's contribution, the term "engagement" might be more accurate than identification. When the spectator engages a film, the experience may be shaped but it is not preordained.

Identification is a concept that is fraught a priori because it is tied to a conception of identity as a wholeness and thus as always ideological. But identity is not the final word on subjectivity. The subject is not simply the identity that it takes up. More fundamentally, it is a desire that emerges when identity falls apart. When feminist film theory focuses solely on identification, it misses the failure of identity and the failure of ideology. By doing so, it paints a picture of ideology that is itself ideological because it offers precious little room for challenging ideology.

Framing the woman's body

One of the lasting contributions of feminist film theory has been its insistence on the significance of how cinema frames the woman's body. Cut up into many pieces, not allowed to actively stride through the landscape, confined to certain spaces, presented in an overly sexual way—the female body in film plays a large part in how we understand women's roles in society. How cinema depicts the female body, feminist film theorists pointed out, plays an essential role in creating the idea of an ideal beauty, which in turn helps to box women in to very limited roles in society.

Early feminist film theorists worked to reveal the way that cinema almost always positions the female body as a sexual object and never a subject (sexual or otherwise). The codes for this may change over the years, but cinema continues to present the female body as an object for men to consume. Representations of men, however, over the history of film, have not had this purpose. While there certainly may be examples of men positioned as sexual objects for women to consume, this is not their primary cinematic role, as it is for women. Film represents men in myriad ways, most often as subject of the frame and the narrative. Certainly, films stereotype men as well as women and pour male characters into various molds of masculinity, but men largely remain in the position of subject rather than object.

The techniques used to film women highlight her object status. For example, directors often frame female characters in a way that highlights certain body parts, such as breasts, hips, or legs. Providing close-ups of her body parts often even before we see her face, the frame cuts her up into fragmented and sexualized objects. In Billy Wilder's *Double Indemnity* (1944), for example, the first time we see Phyllis Dietrichson (Barbara Stanwyck) is from the point of view of Walter Neff (Fred MacMurray), the male protagonist. He has come to the house to sell insurance, and Phyllis appears at the top of the stairs wearing only a towel draped around her. The shot of her occurs from below, from Walter's point of view. The banter between them is sexually charged from the beginning. Phyllis then goes to change—she has been sunbathing—while the camera stays with Walter in the living room where we hear his thought that he would like to see Phyllis again. When she comes down the stairs, which are open on the side with bars, the camera first shows us—in a close-up—her legs in high heels. Since Walter is standing there watching her descend the stairs, we understand that this is his point of view, even though we also understand that he is too far from her to actually see her legs this close up. The spectator interprets this close-up as what Walter is paying attention to rather than what he actually can see. As she finishes walking down the stairs, the camera pans up the rest of her body until it displays her fully and records her finishing buttoning the top of her dress. The film never presents Phyllis's point of view, it never presents her inner thoughts, and it frames her body in this sexualized way throughout. This is a common way to present women in mainstream cinema and one of the aspects of it that feminist film theory has investigated, critiqued, and debated. Embedded in these images is the idea that women enjoy being looked at and derive pleasure from being an object. Coded into this sexual object status are two seemingly contradictory ideas. On the one hand, women have importance as sexual objects. On the other hand, women are not as important or as intellectual or as capable as men because they are nothing but sexual objects. The image of women as mothers, while seemingly different, involves the same contradiction as it proclaims the value of women while simultaneously emphasizing her incapacity for tasks out of the domestic realm.

The problem with cinema's presentation of the body is that we rarely see it even though we look directly at it and accept it. The difficulty in recognizing how the body functions ideologically stems from our association of the body with biology. We think of the body as a biological entity rather than a social or political one. But feminists from Simone de Beauvoir to bell hooks emphasize that the body is an intersection of biology and culture, but this disappears beneath the ideological vision of the body as purely biological. Cinema then employs certain ways of framing the woman's body to codify this naturalization of culture. Initially, feminist film theory attacked Hollywood for cutting the woman up, for representing her in pieces rather than as a whole. Contemporary feminists have questioned this critique by contending that the fragmentation of the body isn't necessarily anti-feminist or ideological. But questions remain: what is a feminist presentation of the female body? How do critics and spectators alike judge representations of female bodies? For feminist film theory, analyzing the framing of the woman's body lays bare many of the fundamental contradictions of femininity.

It is undeniable that the frame provides the foundation for the aesthetics of film, television, and media on the internet. This four-sided frame has the capacity to signify great expanse beyond itself and also to create a sense of utter claustrophobia. How the frame depicts the body can express many things. It can express how spectators should relate to the body. It can express aspects of the character's personality. It can express the character's relationship to other characters or to the environment. As feminist film theorists explored the concept of identification and spectator engagement, they also explored the framing of the woman's body. The critique of identification included within it a critique of how Hollywood framed the woman's body, and just as recent feminist film theory challenged the theory of identification, it has also challenged this position. The shift from feminist film theory in the 1970s to today is not a linear progression by any means. It doesn't evolve from one idea about how to represent the body to some totally new idea. In many ways, this is still a contested issue. But one movement is certain: feminism began by criticizing the use of the female body as a sexual object for male pleasure, and now feminists tend to argue that women should be able to express their sexuality through their sexualized bodies. The feminist project today continues to be to theorize the ramifications of these different positions. Ultimately, the issue of the representation of the woman's body as a sexual object and the woman's expression of sexuality through the body are two different issues, even though at times they become conflated.

The critique of how media employs the female body is still an important critique today. The feminist critique argues that cinema frames the female body as an object instead of as a subject. This is an important critique because the body is a major part of how the subject constitutes itself. Subjects express their relationship to gender, sexuality, culture, and even language through their body. Though we are each born with a particular body, we choose, submit to, rebel against, enjoy, or express ideology through our body. Society asks us to control our bodies, but we can't totally control them. Often our body expresses our unconscious ideas as much as our conscious intentions. As women, for example, we may be angry about having to behave in a certain way, sit in a certain way, eat or talk in a certain way. Yet, at the same time, we might get pleasure or comfort out of these same poses. These contradictory feelings about the relationship between our body and what ideology asks of us make feminism a complex endeavor. How others see us adds to this complexity and has material consequences in our lives. As Simone de Beauvoir says, "woman *is* her body as man *is* his, but her body is something other than her."[16] In other words, the female body comes to represent an idea of femininity that operates in a particular way in society. How one lives in one's body determines one's relationship to femininity, and one feels pressure to align one's body with the ideal. If a woman does not live up to this ideal, she may at best feel ostracized and at worst be perceived as threatening the social order.

The effects of the frame

Feminist theory has long noted the contradictory nature of the ideals of women that dominate patriarchy—namely, woman as sexual object and woman as non-sexual mother. This dichotomy also finds expression in slightly different variations such as whore and virgin or bad girl and good girl. These dichotomies do not line up with the oppositions that we use to describe men, such as hero and villain or cop and criminal. In the realm of popular culture and social fantasy, women don't fit into these male categories. The roles for women—sexual object and mother—have much more rigidity than the male counterparts. Men can transition from one of these categories to the other with relative ease, whereas one has great difficulty imagining a whore becoming a virgin or a mother becoming a sex object.

We can imagine a villain becoming a hero without changing all that much. All he has to do is change his priorities. We can see this in films from Doug Liman's *Bourne Identity* (2002) to Tony Gilroy's *Michael Clayton* (2007) to animated children's film such as Pierre Coffin's *Despicable Me* (2010), in which the main male protagonist starts out as a villain, has a change of heart, and becomes the hero. There are no popular examples of similar transitions in the case of women. We see no prostitutes in Hollywood films who become nurturing mothers or mothers who become prostitutes.

The point is that the different male roles represent different options that the male subject can decide to take up. But for women, the positions of sex object and mother come to define their subjectivity. The constraints on men are not so severe, and the men have significantly more options. Women basically have two choices, and these choices are mutually exclusive. Both positions keep women in the position of an object, while for male characters, it is only a matter of switching subject positions.

These prescribed identities of woman as sexual object or woman as mother contradict each other. One cannot be one and remain the other, and yet, both identities constitute femininity. In this way, the woman always seems incomplete. If she is a mother then she isn't sexual enough, and if she is a sex object then she lacks the nurturing side of femininity. Either way, she can never be whole within the patriarchal fantasy ire and therefore embodies incompletion.

But the woman's incompletion plays a role in the man's possible completion. The patriarchal fantasy envisions the man becoming whole by possessing the woman as an object. The woman participates in wholeness vicariously through the male fantasy that involves her. Possessing the woman provides seemingly complete satisfaction because it offers the illusion of wholeness. In Cameron Crowe's *Jerry Maguire* (1996), this fantasy plays itself out in an almost literal fashion when Jerry Maguire (Tom Cruise) finally tells his love object that he loves her by saying, "You complete me." In other words, the woman, who is herself incomplete, serves as the vehicle for the man simply by acting as a love object.

The idea of the necessary complementarity between men and women motivates these fantasies. Feminism has long worked to reveal the falsity of this image of complementary wholeness by expressing how women don't fit together with men. Feminist slogans such as "A woman needs a man like a fish needs a bicycle" destabilize the idea of complementarity in order to provoke men and women to think about the failure of identity in both sexes. Feminists see it as essential to analyze how the consumption of woman as sexual objects for male pleasure fits into this larger patriarchal fantasy. It both relegates her to object status—denying her the status of subject—while making her the path to completion, happiness, and a fulfilled life. When the camera cuts the female body up into fetishized parts, it expresses this patriarchal fantasy and provides male spectators with the illusion that they could employ these parts as vehicle for their own completion.

Feminist film theorists have sketched out the kinds of female images that film employs in order to make evident the narrow field of roles that women's bodies inhabit. Molly Haskell wrote one of the original texts working in this vein in which she reveals the paucity of character types for women in the cinematic landscape. In *From Reverence to Rape: The Treatment of Women in the Movies*, Haskell surveys the types of female characters from the 1920s to the 1980s that cinema proffered. She begins by saying, "The big lie perpetrated on Western society is the idea of women's inferiority, a lie so deeply ingrained in our social behavior that merely to recognize it is to risk unraveling the entire fabric of civilization."[17] She explains that this leads to limited roles available to women throughout the history of cinema: including women who sacrifice themselves for their family, hypersexualized women, women without any interests besides their interest in men, and so on.

Haskell believes that exposing the narrow range of female roles will raise awareness about how women have been relegated to the position of object. As long as only a few possible female character types exist, there is no possibility for female subjectivity in the cinema. Her work calls for other possibilities for women, and it makes clear that there is a direct relationship between the narrowness of representation and women's oppressed position within society.

Yvonne Tasker later continues theorizing along these same lines. In her *Working Girls: Gender and Sexuality in Popular Cinema* (1998), Tasker provides an updated investigation of types of female characters in Hollywood film in which she concentrates on images of working women. One would think that images of working women, precisely because they are working and not just waiting around for men, would begin to break out of the traditional options laid out for women. And yet, Tasker argues that images of women working follow the pattern of women as sexual objects. Working women, in this sense, mirror the image of the "working girl" or prostitute. In the end, the image of the working woman does not disturb the patriarchal fantasy because of this link. Tasker says, "Across a variety of popular genres, Hollywood representation is characterized by an insistent equation between working women, women's work and some form of sexual(ised) performance."[18] In other words, the working woman still takes up the role of woman as object in film. No matter how active the woman's occupation becomes, she remains a sexual object rather than a desiring subject.

The mother's body

But the other female role, that of the mother, also manifests itself prominently in the cinema. The mother figure is not a subject, but neither is she sexualized. In fact, mothers in cinema have a completely different kind of body than most women. Their bodies nurture, and they exist for the sake of others on the screen. Films encourage the spectator to see the utility of the mother's body but not to desire it.

Theorists such as E. Ann Kaplan and Kathleen Rowe Karilyn have investigated the image of the woman as mother in different moments of cinema's history. E. Ann Kaplan's 1983 investigation into King Vidor's *Stella Dallas* (1937) shows how the mother's body functions as a site of nurturing and thus becomes necessarily disposable. Initially used and then cast aside, Kaplan argues, the mother's body is central to creating new citizens, but only if she fades away afterwards.

Stella Dallas depicts Stella as a single mother who has many suitors and whose working class origins make her stick out in the upper class society to which she aspires. Nonetheless, she perseveres to provide for her daughter, who is eventually wed by an upper class man. In order for this class rising to happen, however, the mother has to step aside. The end of the film, much analyzed by feminist film theorists, provides a frame within a frame. Stella sees her daughter getting married through a large picture window, but she herself does not attend the wedding for fear of embarrassing her daughter. The large window, in the wealthy home, frames the idyllic image of the young beautiful woman in a wedding dress and her attractive man just as they say their vows. A reverse shot away from the window reveals Stella standing in a drab raincoat and hat in the rain, behind a fence that looks like prison bars, staring longingly through the window. Completing the relationship between the two scenes, the camera reverses the shot again to include the window and Stella together. Stella stands below the window as if gazing up at a movie screen watching her daughter get married, a scene she has created, a fantasy she has nurtured, and one in which she constitutively cannot participate.

By taking up her position as excluded female object, Stella is the underside to the image of her daughter in the process of marrying. Kaplan argues that the film positions the mother as the spectator. She says, "And as spectators in the cinema, identifying with the camera, (and thus with Stella's gaze), we learn what it is to be a Mother in patriarchy—it is to renounce, to be on the outside, and to take pleasure in this positioning."[19] These images, Kaplan argues, entrench women into patriarchal fantasy structures. While the film ends with this denigration of the mother, it also provides interesting alternatives in the depiction of Stella's outsider status throughout the film. The spectator watches, as Stella behaves "not lady-like" on the train or in restaurants.

But these are also points of engagement that, while contained in the end, live throughout the rest of the film. Traditional films like this often provided areas of contestation that might have allowed for spectators to enjoy rebellious modes of femininity even if the woman ends up separated from her daughter. But racist images often accompany Stella's rebelliousness. The film depicts Stella's maid in a stereotypically racist manner, and her existence in Stella's life plays a vital role because it gives Stella legitimacy. In other words, the black woman's servitude in this film, which feeds into typical racist images of black women, is used to prop up the white woman's independence. The film offers the depiction of a white female being in charge of her life through the depiction of a black woman as servant, one whose servitude acts as a symbolic marker of class climbing for the white woman. This pits the two women symbolically against each other while at the same time locking white and black femininity into oppositional positions.

The excluded mother's body in *Stella Dallas* has not disappeared in contemporary cinema. According to Kathleen Rowe Karilyn, the mother remains a subservient figure, but the master whom she serves has changed. In *Unruly Girls, Unrepentant Mothers*, Karilyn contends that instead of being subservient to their husbands, mothers in today's cinema are subservient to their children. She argues that the independence of the young woman (who displays "accepted unruliness") is achieved through the rejection of and denigration of the mother. One of her first examples is James Cameron's *Titanic* (1997) in which the daughter must reject the mother in order to free herself from the chains of patriarchal society, which the mother represents.

Because the woman's freedom depends on breaking from the mother, contemporary feminism has had an ambivalent relationship to representations of mothers. The mother becomes an ambivalent figure. Karilyn says: "My purpose is to consider the ways feminism has absorbed this ambivalence when, in renewing itself, it has distanced itself from the generations that preceded it, thereby replicating that very misogyny it wishes to eradicate."[20] Karilyn points out that though popular culture certainly has changed in reaction to feminism and changing expectations about women, the depiction of mothers in today's popular culture reveals a new yet similar structural place for the image of the mother as the flip side to the depiction of the sexual woman as object.

The mother's body avoids the sexualization that most women's bodies undergo in cinema. But it remains an object nevertheless. Patriarchal ideology conceives the mother as one side of femininity, and even though this side plays less of a role on film than the sex object, it is necessary. The sex object depends on the mother, which is why feminist film theory has focused on both.

Disturbances of the frame

Feminist film theorists have looked at the way that film has molded the female body into particular character types, each of which has a certain way of dressing and a certain bodily look. These types repeat themselves throughout genres and cultural movements. Feminist film theorists have also made note of other key trends in film in relation to the female body. If most filmic trends depict female bodies in roles that fulfill a patriarchal fantasy, Barbara Creed, in her influential 1993 study of women in horror films, illuminated ways that the female body holds the key to patriarchal nightmares as well.[21] In *Monstrous Feminine*, Creed investigates not only female character types that repeat in horror films but also how the monstrous feminine appears in the mise-en-scène.[22] The fear of femininity manifests itself even in settings and props, according to Creed. Engaging French feminist theorist Julia Kristeva's theories of the feminine and the abject, Creed illuminates the way patriarchal hatred and fear of women informs US horror films.

Creed explains that the maternal body, the act of giving birth, and even menstruation find their way into the setting of horror films. Ridley Scott's *Alien* (1979), for example, depicts the commercial spacecraft *Nostromo* returning home after a long voyage. The *Nostromo* investigates a distress signal and finds a wrecked ship on a planet. Inside the ship, the crew discovers a chamber containing thousands of oblong objects. The mise-en-scène, Creed points out, includes shapes and structures reminiscent of female genitalia and the womb. In addition, the chamber with the egg objects contains oozing mucous all around, and when one of the eggs opens, it drips with this mucous. The film has other images of oozing material as part of the horror that lurks around every corner. Examining these representations of the feminine, Creed says: "She is there in the images of birth, the representations of the primal scene, the womb-like imagery, the long winding tunnels leading to inner chambers, the rows of hatching eggs, the body of the mother-ship, the voice of the life-support system, and the birth of the alien."[23] Creed argues that this imagery embodies the "monstrous feminine." In this way, the uncontrollable part of femininity defines the alien's otherness.

By centering horror films on the monstrous feminine, Hollywood registers the capacity of women to disrupt the cinematic frame. Rather than containing femininity in a specified role, horror films often show it breaking out of control. The depiction of femininity as a nightmare in horror films runs counter to the standard depiction of the woman as a fantasy object. Even though the feminine is associated with negativity, it nonetheless breaks the bounds of the patriarchal frame.

Feminist film theorists have also responded to the stereotypes of femininity in cinema by seeking out male images that disrupt the patriarchal frame. For example, Kaja Silverman's *Male Subjectivity at the Margins* considers the way "deviant" masculinities, expressed through depictions of the male body in cinema, can say "no" to patriarchal power. These male bodies resist mainstream masculinity through undefined desire that manifests itself visually either in the wounded male body or the enjoying male body—both of which are not mainstream masculine depictions. These images of the wounded, uncontrollable, unpredictable male body lead her to conclude that "unconscious desire and identification do not always follow the trajectory delineated for them in advance, and that they sometimes assume forms which are profoundly antipathetic to the existing social formation."[24] For Silverman, films mark these male bodies through their visual presentation and position them as a stain in the image rather than a controller of a masterful look. In this sense, their bodies represent this "no" both on their flesh and in how they are placed in the mise-en-scène.[25]

Recent scholarship on the male melodrama considers similar resistances to the social order through the image of the male body. These studies take up Silverman's interest in male bodies on screen that present a "de-idealization and mutilation of the male body."[26] Feminist postcolonial theorist Hyon Joo Yoo, for example, sees this presented in recent Korean films. She argues that through the formal presentation of the male body a "moribund masculinity" becomes a space of resistance against dominant ideas of nationalism. About the character Jeon Tae-il (Hong Kyeong-in) in Pak Kwang-Su's *A Single Spark* (1995), for instance, she says: "In representing masculinity through an unrecuperable death that does not yield a masculine myth, Pak constructs a cinematic aesthetics that can be translated into a counter-capitalist symbolic economy as a departure point of cultural resistance." [27] Yoo investigates how cinema represents male bodies as fractured subjects more than whole bodies; they are bodies with contradictions that are impossible to define and become a site of resistance.

This focus on the male body follows from feminist film theory's attempt to discern potential sites of weakness within the patriarchal frame. If masculinity is not whole, then the feminine can break from the confines of the frame. The vulnerability of the masculine body attests to the vulnerability of patriarchal ideology. Feminist film theorists constantly looked for new ways to challenge this ideology and its conception of the female body, and the evolution of these challenges often coincided with changes in feminist practice.

Women reframing their own bodies

Though feminist film theory spent much time critiquing the sexualized female body on screen, later feminist film theorists began to see sexualized depictions of the body differently. Understanding the contradictory nature of the subject allows us to see the body as a potential site of expression of this contradiction. Embodying this contradiction turns the body into a site of resistance. Specifically, the body can resist the prevailing ideology, which normally works to cover over contradiction. One of the biggest shifts in the image of the female body occurred around seeing the sexualized female body as potentially a site of resistance.

To analyze this, one must first understand the shift from second to third wave feminism. Third wave feminism called for a new feminism that included all women and men interested in equality. This new wave of feminism emerged out of the feeling that second wave feminism by the 1990s seemed outdated and no longer viable. Additionally, feminism received a great deal of bad press in the mainstream media, and young women wanted to present a new image of what it meant to be a feminist. Rather than taking up the critical attitude that second wave feminism had toward images of sexualized femininity, third wave feminism embraced female sexualization as empowering. This is not to say that third wave feminism abandoned critique. It consisted largely of young women in the 1990s and 2000s who became activists on issues like sexual abuse or worked to form a radical girl culture. The 1990s "riot grrrl" bands are a good example of this new feminism.

The riot grrrl bands were an underground music scene that came out of indie rock but often addressed such issues as rape, patriarchy, racism, domestic abuse, and sexual orientation directly, as well as providing a culture in which women could pursue music without the constraints of the male dominated music world. They also created an entire subculture involving zines, art, and political activism. The name riot grrrl came from a combination of band members' oft-used terms, including the reinvention of "girl." Men, especially men in power, often employed the word "girl" as a belittling term for women. The new grrrl—with a growl—changed the word while adding an implicit critique and empowerment. Third wave feminists often reclaimed hurtful terms as a symbol of their political intentions. Rather than eschewing words such as "bitch" and "slut" because they injured women psychically, these feminists took them up with pride as symbols of empowerment and forms of political action.

Bitch magazine remains the most public example of this reclamation process. The tag line of this magazine explains its mission as "a feminist response to pop culture." The magazine began as an alternative to the feminist magazine *Ms.*, which functioned as the lodestar for second wave feminism. *Ms.* references the salutation for women that did not refer to marital status. Rather than being called "Miss" before marriage and "Mrs." after marriage, women in the second wave often adopted the salutation "Ms." in order to signify that their identity did not consist in their relationship to marriage. The change in connotation from *Ms.*, first appearing in 1971, to *Bitch*, first appearing in 1996, serves as a good example of the shift between second and third wave feminism. In many ways, the magazines are similar since they both have had issues that concentrated on politics and on readings of popular culture. But the difference lies in how they interpret the efficacy of political critique.

Ms. aims at creating a new space in the social order for women, one that is not defined by their relationship to men. The magazine claims a rarely utilized term to signify independence and self-respect. The term "Ms." attempts to change the symbolic terrain. That is to say, it attempts to change the codes of behavior and belief systems in order to create equality between genders in this system. *Bitch* magazine, on the other hand, implicitly reacts to what the editors see as the failure of this kind of symbolic political activism involving the term "Ms.". By the mid-1990s, the feminism of the second wave had had a significant effect on culture but had not effected as much change as women had hoped. Backlash in the media, the corporate world, and in the justice system to feminist issues played a role in the dampening of change. Court decisions and pressure on clinics throughout the United States had steadily eroded the hard-won right to an abortion, for example. And though many more women were now attending college and graduate school, a glass ceiling became evident, and it prevented women from instituting significant change in the social power hierarchy.

Additionally young women were still being harassed and put down by terms such as "bitch," often when they tried to assert themselves. The vituperative response of calling women names such as "bitch" or "slut" is an attempt to destroy the woman's symbolic position and warn them to take up a more subdued subservient position. One uses these terms to express an irrational aggression, which also expresses a structural attempt to oppress women. The founders of *Bitch*, now called

Bitch Media, explain this on their website. They say, "we stand firm in our belief that if we choose to reappropriate the word, it loses its power to hurt us. And if we can get people thinking about what they're saying when they use the word, that's even better."[28] In this way, the magazine editors see reappropriation of a hurtful word as a way to air out the obscene underside, that irrational aggression, and rob it of its power.

The question remains whether this is a successful strategy. Certainly, the appearance of a fourth wave of feminism that does not seem to be emphasizing reappropriation as a political strategy in the same way suggests that this approach is receding into the past. Words such as "bitch" and "slut" have apparently worked their way into girl culture today, and yet it remains unclear whether the words have the effect of empowerment or degradation. Indeed in many social arenas, these words continue to retain the aggression and violence that they had in the past. For feminism, the question of the efficacy of reappropriation remains an important one. It acts as a kind of quilting point for the debates about how to wrestle with popular culture in a way that provokes people into thinking through culture's ramifications. This debate is not just about words but also about images.[29]

Perhaps the defining feature of third wave feminism is its attempt to reappropriate the sexualized female body. Specifically, third wave feminism and riot grrrl culture often disrupted mainstream ways of thinking about the female body: sometimes in traditional feminist ways (by rejecting feminine styles) and sometimes in the spirit of what *Bitch* magazine tries to do (by reappropriating sexist feminine styles). Riot grrrls dressed in a unique style that brought together elements of punk, heavy metal, grunge, and butch lesbian but never had any one set theme. Nonetheless, self-expression through style was a key part of the movement. Many third wave feminists and riot grrrls felt that second wave feminism's theories about the dangers of female objectification were also positions against sexual attire. Riot grrrls often emphasized their sexuality but in a more aggressive and anti-mainstream manner. For example, they might wear a catholic schoolgirl shirt with a short skirt, punk boots, and punk hair. Juxtaposing different stereotypes of femininity became a way to confront those stereotypes while potentially expressing something new. Just as the movement worked to reclaim hurtful terms, it also worked to reclaim the female body as a sexual object.

This attempt came out of feminism's claim that the mainstream media lack any depictions of female pleasure. Popular culture and music tend to emphasize images of women as fantasies in order to facilitate male pleasure. Even images of women enjoying sex appear only within a male fantasy of what that enjoyment looks like.[30] Riot grrrls implicitly and explicitly worked to make female pleasure central. For the riot grrrls, women playing guitar, banging the drums, and aggressively singing announced their own pleasure. Riot grrrls also wrote words such as "slut" and "rape" across their bodies while they performed in order to call attention to the sexual violence done to the female body. This act politicized their actual bodies by turning the body itself into a signifier that informed how the society sees it. Not everyone understood this critique, and at times the mainstream media understood the movement as young women explicitly courting violence and sex. This only further emphasized the points these bands were making. That is to say, these bands—and the third wave movements in general—saw the female body as the battleground for female oppression but also as its potential greatest source of empowerment. Rather than making themselves look un-feminine, they combined myriad styles to create a new alternative, one that expressed pleasure and enjoyment without reference to any male fantasy. This eclectic style became an emblem of third wave feminism.

Some feminists see categorizing feminism into waves as unhelpful because it creates a culture of antagonism between generations rather than building coalitions. Others, however, are already calling for a discussion of fourth wave feminism. People discuss fourth wave feminism in reference to two developments. Firstly, for many, the impact of the internet on feminism defines the fourth wave. From 2010 to 2015, the internet has played a large role in the feminist activism of younger women and their experience of feminism in general. Secondly, fourth wave feminism calls for feminism with more diversity. While intersectionality, critical race theory, queer theory, transgender theory, and more, came into being during third wave feminism, they have had only a limited impact on the third wave. Theorists and activists have criticized the third wave and feminists like the riot grrrls for a lack of diversity.

Each wave starts with the hope of more inclusiveness. The second wave wanted to include popular culture and the domestic sphere; the third wave wanted to include more frank discussions of race and sexuality; and the fourth wave wants to include queer and transgender identities. Rather than seeing each wave as a movement that failed, it might be helpful to view the creation of new feminist movements as young feminists trying to better address the concerns of their time while dealing with the controlling nature of patriarchy. Each new wave deals with the restrictions that women still encounter within patriarchy. Each wave emerges out of the cultural, political, and sociological changes of their historical moment. For third and fourth wave feminism, for example, the September 11, 2001 attacks on the United States and the subsequent wars in Afghanistan and Iraq fundamentally changed the domestic landscape. The Patriot Act and other internal policing actions, done in the name of national security, impacted culture as a whole by creating more paranoia.

Often people's response to the trauma of the attacks and the trauma of the ongoing war (including the loss of life, the revelation of the use of torture, and so on) is to go back to traditional patriarchal ideas. Feminist journalist Susan Faludi, for example, documents women losing their jobs from careers as disparate as broadcasting to firefighting following the attacks, as a traumatized nation regressed in its gender politics. Faludi argues: "Taken individually, the various impulses that surfaced after 9/11—the denigration of capable women, the magnification of manly men, the heightened call for domesticity, the search for and sanctification of helpless girls— might seem a random expression of some profound cultural derangement."[31] She goes on to explain that seen together the responses reveal a national myth of invincibility that was shaken. She documents the way that the media and politicians reacted to the attacks by re-establishing women into the domestic sphere through their rhetoric and representations, as well as in hiring practices. Her book *The Terror Dream* suggests that the September 11, 2001 attacks and the ensuing wars had a profound effect on the state of feminism. The expansion of the internet and the dominance of social media today, which has entirely changed the way we communicate with each other, may have similarly impacted gender politics and social relations. To be able to engage the changing political landscape, feminism must be a way of engaging and theorizing world changes—a way of theorizing a culture that often thrives on being unaware of itself.

Framing the actress

Feminist film theory today can engage the media industry, which is such an essential part of the changing political landscape, by promoting an intersectional way of theorizing that takes into account desire, loss, and anxiety while theorizing the relationship between the particular and the universal of identity. In this sense, feminism must embody a questioning stance that grapples with the contradictions of identity. Articulating the contradictions of identity is the primary feminist challenge today, and this provides a way of analyzing how Hollywood functions as an industry as well as the films that it produces.

The Academy Awards stand as a good example of Hollywood's concerns and ideological positions. Its telecasts throughout the past decades certainly display the current trends in female beauty and expectations of female behavior. The Oscars telecast puts female beauty on display for hundreds of millions of people to see. Analyzing the show reveals the importance of theorizing the contradictions of identity that work to define the women on stage and in the films. This annual awards show for film remains one of the few live television events that garner huge audiences around the world.

The show often works to cover over the traumas and failures of the year's films while celebrating its accomplishments. The nominations, awards given, jokes made, star appearances, and so on, take on cultural importance and reveal the political disjunctures of the time. This is true of the minutiae of the show, but it is also true of the more eventful political moments. Oftentimes, through a critical analysis or through an event at the show, the tensions between representation and politics become quite evident. Or rather the relation between the film industry and the political landscape becomes evident. During this moment, it becomes apparent that the intersections of identities also reveal the fissures in ideology. For example, in an unprecedented move, at the 2003 Academy Awards presentation Michael Moore invited all his nominated colleagues on stage with him when his *Bowling for Columbine* (2003) won for best documentary. *Bowling for Columbine* investigates violence in the United States and its relation to our national identity. With the nominated group standing by him, he criticized George Bush's election and Bush waging war in Iraq for fictitious reasons.[32] Horrified by this display of open conflict, the producers shut him down and whisked him off stage before he could finish talking. His actions and words clearly surprised the producers of the show as well as the audience but became a well-known moment of public dissension. The act also suggested that the purpose of political art was to take up a questioning stance in relation to national myths. This political act revealed both the fissures in the political ideology of that time as well as the role that Hollywood felt it had in relation to that ideology.

Sexism and racism in the United States—and their prevalence in Hollywood—has also long been on display in the Academy Awards. Most obviously, women of all colors and black men rarely receive nominations and even more rarely win best director, cinematographer, screenwriter, best picture, and so on. The first woman awarded best director was white, and this award was only in 2012. Only three other white women have been nominated for best director (Lena Wertmüller, *Seven Beauties* [1976], Jane Campion, *The Piano* [1993], and Sophia Coppola, *Lost in Translation* [2010]). As of 2015, no black director has won for best director and only three black men have been nominated (John Singleton, *Boyz n the Hood* [1991], Lee Daniels *Precious* [2009], Steve McQueen, *12 Years a Slave* [2013]).

The lack of equality in the awards remains a marker for the active racist and sexist mindset of the individuals who bestow Academy Awards and of the film industry within which they work. Stars who receive an award often respond to these discrepancies. Halle Berry, for example, was the first black actress to receive an academy award for Best Actress in a Leading Role. She received this award in 2001, the 74th Oscars show, for her role in *Monsters Ball* (2000). When she accepted the award she said, "This moment is so much bigger than me. This moment is for Dorothy Dandridge, Lena Horne, Diahann Carroll. It's for the women that stand beside me, Jada Pinkett, Angela Bassett, Vivica Fox. And it's for every nameless, faceless woman of color that now has a chance because this door tonight has been opened." This statement acknowledges several important aspects of theorizing feminism and film. On the one hand, Berry points to the history of the erasure of black women from films in general. On the other hand, she makes it clear that she sees herself in solidarity with the other black actresses out there working hard to fight a very rigid system. And she also highlights the way that Hollywood erases the singularity of black women and in doing this erases singularity as such.

Film continues to be a medium that employs very few characters to tell a story; it focuses often on less than a handful of characters. The rest of the characters have less depth and serve as extras or side characters. Black female characters, when they appear in films at all, often occupy positions that render them nameless and faceless and thus devoid of singularity. Berry highlights this in her speech as she hopes that her win will make it better for all black actresses by opening the minds of filmmakers and the purses of Hollywood. But a solitary win does not always have the effect of opening the gate that award winners might hope. As of 2015, fifteen years after Berry's win, no other black actress has won the award.[33]

At times, like Michael Moore, stars have also used the moment of their acceptance speech to make other kinds of political statements. Such was the case for Patricia Arquette accepting the Best Supporting Actress for her work in Richard Linklater's *Boyhood* (2014). In her acceptance speech, she chose to highlight the importance for women to have equal pay, and it elicited a strong applause from the audience. With her speech, she intended to make a feminist intervention into the awards ceremony and into the culture at large. Arquette clearly thought out her strategy, as evinced by the paper that she brought to the stage and read directly from throughout the entire time. Her determination also manifested itself in her firm, almost shaking, grip on the paper, as well as her determined attitude to read it all until she was finished.

The media's treatment of Arquette leading up to the awards was further evidence of the sexist standards of ideal femininity since they often focused mostly on her body. The reporters did celebrate her performance in *Boyhood*, but they also always mentioned her bravery in taking a role in which she would have to age in front of the camera. The film took place over twelve years of a young boy's life, and Linklater purposefully took twelve years to shoot the film. The aging of the actors themselves was part of the mise-en-scène of the film. This element of the film fascinated audiences and created interest in what was otherwise a slow-moving and uneventful film. Not having plastic surgery and allowing her natural body to age from her thirties into her forties was, by Hollywood standards, a radical act, and critics received it as such. For example, Cara Buckley from the *New York Times* wrote: "She also did something quietly revolutionary for a Hollywood actress: Over the dozen years of *Boyhood*, she unapologetically and naturally aged on-screen, her body widening and her face adding wrinkles as she grew into middle age."[34] For this reporter and many others, Arquette's wrinkles and widening body was in fact news. This shows the extent to which the patriarchal idea of female beauty continues to hold sway in popular culture. In case it is not evident enough, this example proves that in the patriarchal fantasy most often played out on the screen the female body has only a very few rigid types it is supposed to fit into, and aging does not fit into this fantasy.

Arquette was well aware of this and often explained that aging on screen was one of the things that attracted her to the role. She wanted to move beyond the sexy ingénue role that Hollywood had put her into, which she found unrealistic. Her feminist statement clearly matched her well-considered choice of this role. Her argument for equal pay for equal work fit into this attempt to break down the patriarchal structure of Hollywood. But Arquette's attack on patriarchy took a strange turn when she left the stage.

On stage she argued for all women to have equal pay for equal work. Backstage, however, reporters asked Arquette to comment further, and she said: "It's time for all women in America and all the men who love women and all the gay people and people of color that we've all fought for to fight for us now."[35] This comment backstage retroactively changed the meaning of what she said on stage. Her backstage comments separated "gay people" and "people of color" from women, and thus it became clear that when she spoke on stage, she meant primarily straight white women, even if her words didn't make this explicit. Many reporters the following day, especially from feminist news sources, pointed out that women were also gay and of color. Arquette's comments harkened back to the feminism of the 1970s in which white women argued for feminism but often made it clear that they were fighting exclusively for white women. Arquette's backstage comments revealed her blindness to the intersectional nature of identity, once again erasing women of color and queer women from the definition of woman.

This type of thinking damages the feminist project of gender equality because it presents gender as an isolated identity that applies only to certain women. It also suggests that female identity is whole rather than acknowledging the fractured nature of identity as such. On the one hand, it is tempting to peg Arquette as a second or third wave feminist who doesn't understand the needs of our contemporary situation. On the other hand, it would be more productive to see what it is that her statement gets wrong about identity. In this sense, feminism could theorize the way that the contradictions of identity evident during this show encourage a questioning response to Arquette, including why are these identities seen at odds and what do her words reveal about ideology and its current depiction of women?

Arquette's performance both on and off stage at the Academy Awards offers insight into the contemporary dilemma that confronts feminist theory. It must be universalizing in order to have any political effect at all, and at the same time, it must account for the particular variations within the universal. The only way to accomplish this is to grasp identity itself as thoroughly based in contradiction: one never is fully a woman because the identity is at odds with itself. By emphasizing that no one wholly belongs, we allow everyone space to be a part of the feminist project.

Who framed feminism?

In addition to the announcement of a fourth feminist wave, others have proclaimed that a epoch of post-feminism followed the third wave. The mantra of post-feminism ironically represented an attempt to develop feminism further and to escape some of the difficulties that have beset earlier iterations of feminism. At times, the third wave has taken up this term, but more often theorists separate post-feminism from the waves of feminism. Usually, it holds negative connotations—feminists lament that we live in a post-feminist world—but there are also women who take up the term as a positive way to reinvent feminism. Most often, theorists employed it to describe the sexualized yet powerful woman of the 1990s and 2000s.

Post-feminism, however, never developed into a defined set of political or theoretical ideas. Similarly, media outlets used it to encompass disparate ideas: simply a time after feminism, the connotation that feminism is no longer needed, or as an alternative to feminism. *Time* magazine famously ran a cover story on June 29, 1998 with the title "Is Feminism Dead?" and a photo of four women (Susan B. Anthony, Betty Friedan, Gloria Steinem, and lastly a television character named Ally McBeal [Calista Flockhart]). The irony here—appropriate to our current discussion—is that the final woman who marks the end of feminism in this magazine cover is a fictional television character. *Ally McBeal* was one in a string of television series and films that focused on women who seemed to embody the idea of post-feminism. Specifically, they reaped the benefits of feminism through their high paying jobs as well as their access to careers that were previously closed to women. And yet, they claimed they themselves were not feminist. Additionally, they often performed a certain kind of sexuality and feminine style. These characters also expressed their independence through their ability to shop, an activity that once connoted female dependence. Critics often categorized this brand of feminism as consumer feminism.

Sex and the City (1998–2004) is the quintessential example of this consumer feminism. The female characters took great pleasure in buying beautiful shoes that cost six hundred to a thousand dollars. The show also depicted women having sex for their own pleasure but then entwined this with these same women conforming themselves to the ideal beauty standards. The shoes that they valued—extreme high heels—emerged directly from the patriarchal fantasy of ideal female beauty. The reason women wear these shoes is that society makes them feel as if they look sexier and prettier when they are wearing them, that they approach ideal beauty more completely. Women have internalized the idea that their legs look skinnier and more attractive when they are in high heels. But consumer feminism or post-feminism presents wearing high heels as a badge of feminist emancipation.

On screen, women must play out this aspect of ideal beauty. Women from Jennifer Lopez to Jennifer Anniston to Halle Berry have all donned extremely high heels in the roles they take on. The look has become a marker of wealthy powerful women, as well as a marker of feminine sexuality itself, and few can resist its appeal. Even action heroines are depicted performing athletic heroic feats in their high heels. Beyond being unrealistic, this emphasizes that whatever else these women are they will always be marked by this signifier that assures audiences that they are indeed still sexual objects.[36]

The persistence of high heels on the screen signifies the recalcitrance of the patriarchal frame for the woman's body. Though women have moved into leading parts in many popular films and television shows, their bodies remain framed in traditional ways. Popular culture has not provided a satisfactory response to the challenge of feminist theory, which is why many feminist film theorists have turned to female auteurs in search of a film equal to feminism's theorizing.

The female auteur

Throughout the history of film theory, many feminists have looked to female filmmakers to offer alternatives to the plethora of patriarchal depictions of women that all the waves of feminism have tried to analyze. While not all female filmmakers see themselves as feminist, feminist film theorists often argue that these filmmakers indeed present new possibilities. Feminist film theorists from Laura Mulvey to Valerie Smith to Christina Lane often saw a different aesthetic emerging among female filmmakers despite what these filmmakers said about themselves.[37]

Female directed films certainly did provide insight into alternative representations of women, but it also confounded feminist film theorists as well. Sigmund Freud once said about his discovery of the unconscious that the poets knew it first. One might argue the same of female filmmakers, whose work might not have followed the feminism of the day exactly and yet challenged the patriarchal status quo nonetheless. Female directed films often presented formal and narrative structures that emphasized female pleasure, female pursuits, and the contradiction of identity.

It is important to begin by distinguishing between the female filmmaker and the female auteur. Certainly, every female filmmaker could be a female auteur, but many do not have the chance. It is just as important to analyze female filmmakers work who only make one or two films, but it is also essential to advocate for women to have long careers as directors. In its basic form, auteur theory lays out a way to understand the role of the director as author of the film. More than this, however, when the films of an auteur are studied as a group, the thematic and stylistic repetitions reveal the larger ideas of the auteur and of her films. Film theorist Peter Wollen explains: "[Filmmaker Jean] Renior once remarked that a director spends his whole life making one film; this film, which it is the task of the critic to construct, consists not only of the typical features of its variants, which are merely its redundancies, but of the principle of variation which governs it, that is its esoteric structure, which can only manifest itself or 'seep to the surface,' in Lévi-Strauss's phrase, 'through the repetition process.'"[38] Thinking about filmmakers as auteurs allows theorists to grapple with the conscious and unconscious choices of the filmmaker as well as the structural repetitions that express both the individual filmmaker and the social order within which they are producing.

The female auteur as a category brings up larger feminist concerns. First among them is the veritable dearth of female auteurs. There are not many female auteurs because female filmmakers do not receive the same support that male filmmakers receive. Additionally, the majority of female filmmakers with long careers and a plethora of films do not work in Hollywood, and this limits the visibility of their films and the amount of money that they have to make films. Auteurs such as Jane Campion (Australia), Claire Denis (France), Agnès Varda (France), Margarethe von Trotta (Germany), Mira Nair (India), just to name a few, do not base their work in the United States and often receive funding from their home nation. Working in Hollywood for women remains difficult, but establishing a long career of many films is even more difficult. A long career allows for investigation of a specific vision, it allows for failure as well as success, and it allows for interpretations of the world from various stages of one's life as an artist.

Women directors in Hollywood sometimes have the chance to make a film or two, but they very rarely have the chance to make feature length films over their whole career. In "The Celluloid Ceiling," Martha Lauzen reports that in 2014, for example, of the 250 top box office films women directed only 7 percent of these films.[39] The study also notes that this is 2 percent less than in 1998, which indicates that women are not making progress in Hollywood. The ramifications of this are extensive. With so few women granted funds for feature length films each year—the study, for example, considers a stretch of sixteen years—it is less likely that any single female director will have the chance to have a long career as a director.

Many directors who make one to three films eventually move to television or other roles in the film industry because they cannot find support for further films. The low percentage of women given budgets reinforces the lack of female auteurs. Significantly, this also impacts the representation of women. Of the top one hundred films from 2014, females comprised only 30 percent of speaking roles and only 12 percent of protagonists.[40] The statistics show that women directors, producers, and screenwriters create more speaking female characters and female protagonists. Access to key roles in the industry for women has a clear impact on representation in general.

Filmmakers and scholars often look to auteurs to define certain styles, genres, and societal concerns. For example, Alfred Hitchcock's oeuvre has a tremendous impact on the suspense genre. His interpretation of suspense, the qualities of a good villain, and the way women function within that genre are authoritative. Similarly, Spike Lee's films with their visually innovative investigation into popular culture and intense critique of ideology shape films about one's identity in relation to one's community, black identity in the United States, and interracial relationships. Or consider John Ford's legacy. His many films, even after years of critique about their gender and racial politics, still influence filmmakers making westerns as well as depictions of the male hero.

These auteurs developed their ideas over many films and several decades. With each film they worked through their central concerns and political, aesthetic, or narrative ideas. They each had films that didn't do well at the box office as well as films that critics didn't praise, and yet they continued to receive funding for more films, which enabled their vision. It is through this evolution that they were able to impact the film world and popular culture. It is important to note that there are also few black directors that become auteurs. Spike Lee is one of the few in the United States, and he certainly hasn't received the same kind of monetary support that white male auteurs often receive in Hollywood. There are individual films that have impacted the film world, but the unconscious desire, intellectual ideas, and artistic innovation entwined into a general approach to filmmaking that the audience encounters with the auteur has a lasting impact. Yet in the landscape of film auteurs, there are very few female voices. The implications of this lack remain far-reaching.

Without the voices of female auteurs, the filmmaking landscape remains completely one-sided. It might be that female auteurs would not affect the sexist imagery that populates this landscape, as they too would be bound to the patriarchal whims of the box office, but we cannot know this until there are an equal number of female voices present. Considering what female filmmakers produce and what the few female auteurs work on, it is likely that a real presence would indeed affect the gender equity in representation. As feminist media pundits are rightly fond of saying, there are an equal number of women in society and in the audience, thus there should be an equal number of female filmmakers, female speaking roles, and female protagonists. Again, there is no way of knowing what this would look like, but most likely it would look different than what we have now. By engaging the work of two female auteurs (Jane Campion and Julie Dash), I will sketch out some of the innovative interventions that female auteurs have made into such topics as spectator engagement, the framing of the female body, and the representation of female pleasure.

Female auteur: Jane Campion

Jane Campion, born in New Zealand but based in Australia, is the second of four women ever nominated for the Academy Award for Best Director, and she is also the first female filmmaker to ever receive the Palme D'Or (the highest prize given at the Cannes Film Festival), which she won for *The Piano* (1993). She made her first film, a short film called *Peel*, in 1992 and to date has made seven features and a television series (of six episodes). Campion's films all have women at the center of the narrative. She often writes original screenplays for her films, and does not always follow standard narrative trajectories. Her narratives at times meander more than the traditional linear narrative. In part, this is because Campion seems to follow the adventures and choices of her female character, which inevitably take them off the beaten path of expected trajectories for women within a patriarchal society.

Her films are about women who have a passion, for example, writing (in *An Angel at My Table*, 1990), or piano playing (in *The Piano*), or words themselves (in *In the Cut*, 2003). Their passion defines who they are and the choices that they make, but it is not a typical passion. It is not a passion that is meant to lead them to fame or fortune but rather her films investigate women devoted to their everyday passions. In this way, Campion's films are about the radicalism of the seemingly mundane devotions.[41]

The women in Campion's films often upset the social order by being true to their passions. Her films suggest that simply valuing female desire and pleasure can have radical effects. The visual style of Campion's films works with the narrative in fascinating ways. Early on in her filmmaking career, she collaborated with cinematographer Sally Bongers. Together they created a unique and meaningful mise-en-scène, linked together with unexpected camera angles and color schemes. Though this collaboration ended after Campion's first feature film, *Sweetie* (1989), Campion continued this practice throughout her career. In all of her films, she expresses the experiences of the main female character through the form of the film itself. Whether it is in tone, color, deceptive point of view shots, or unique mise-en-scène, her films express the subjectivity of her main character. In the film *In the Cut*, Campion even goes so far as to have the focus fade in and out over the screen to suggest when her main character is fully experiencing her great love of words.

Campion reveals and expresses her female characters by showing their point of view, but more often she also shows them in their landscape to express their relation to the social order. She often shoots her female characters in full form and while she may have close-ups of them, she does not sexualize these close-ups. At times, the main close-ups that focus on the female body are of their hands engaging in what they are passionate about, such as playing the piano or writing, or the close-ups focus on their eyes as they look at people or things. This transforms the close-up of the female body away from the patriarchal norm of the objectified close-up functioning only to further sexualize the female in a way that fits into a male fantasy. Campion's close-up instead rejuvenates the female body by presenting it as both creative and pleasurable. In this sense, the parts of the body are portrayed as the source of inspiration and fascination for the women themselves.

Campion investigates female desire and pleasure throughout all of her films in similarly creative ways, which in turn challenge traditional male depictions of female sexuality and sex. Her women express their desire and enjoy their bodies. The men involved with Campion's women either find the women's desire destabilizing, or they reveal themselves not to be typical male lovers. For example, in *In the Cut*, Frannie Avery's (Meg Ryan) lover Giovanni Malloy (Mark Ruffalo) reveals that an older woman taught him to be a good lover. Her relationship to her own body transformed him, and he clearly values this as an important part of his personality. Campion's depictions of female pleasure obliterate the complementary relationship of women as object and men as subject. Men and women are not complementary in Campion's films, but they do experience pleasure together and interact as equals.

In all of Campion's films, there is a scene in which somewhere in the background there is a woman in a wedding dress. Her characters never get married and yet this image haunts the films like a specter at the edge of the frame, one that is resisted but clearly present. In this way, Campion suggests that these patriarchal expectations haunt all women as they grow up, engage with the world, and find their passions and the things that they will devote themselves to but also that they have to live with the contradictions that these expectations often pose in relation to their own desires. In considering her films relation to the woman's film, film theorist Hilary Radner sees this theme of contradiction in Campion's films in general. She says: "In this sense, Campion offers a contemporary version of the woman's film that foregrounds the problem of contradiction and of film's inability to reconcile that contradiction—because the adult world requires the acceptance of loss (within the cinema of Campion)."[42] Radner here makes an important point that Campion reveals film's unique ability to present contradiction.

Campion films imply that stories from a female point of view highlight the contradictions embedded in the social order. French feminist filmmaker Catherine Breillat also addresses this when she says, "cinema is a mode of expression that allows you to express all the nuances of a thing while including its opposites. These are things that can't be quantified mentally; yet they can exist and be juxtaposed. That may seem very contradictory. Cinema allows you to film these contradictions."[43] As international independent female directors, Breillat and Campion have the freedom to explore how the contradictions of being female in a patriarchal order can be expressed through the unique nature of film form. Through the specter of the woman in a wedding dress, Campion allows this image to create tension within her scene without explaining why it is there, she creates layers within the image that prompt the spectator to engage with the films in multiple ways. US director Julie Dash also expresses identity through allowing contradiction to inhabit the frame rather than trying to cover it up.

Female auteur: Julie Dash

Julie Dash was born and raised in New York City but went to UCLA for an MFA in Film and Television Production. The Library of Congress named her film *Daughters of the Dust* (1991) to the National Film Registry in 2004. It was also the first feature length film by a black female filmmaker to receive a general theatrical release in the United States. She has made numerous award winning short films and five feature length films. Women filmmakers in the United States have historically had a very difficult time getting studios to support their films, and black women filmmakers have an even more difficult time. Had Dash been making films in another country she may well have had the financial and infrastructural support that a filmmaker like Jane Campion had from Australia. Nonetheless, her body of work is large enough to layout her vision, and her influence on the US independent film scene has been significant. Her short film *Illusions* (1982) and her feature length film *Daughters of the Dust* both present black female characters in vastly different ways than the US mainstream film industry. Her inventive framing of the female body and her intricate narrative structures have garnered attention worldwide providing alternative ways of presenting female bodies.

Illusions is a short film that depicts a day in the life of Mignon Dupree (Lonette McKee), a black female producer in Hollywood in 1942. As the narrative moves on, the film reveals that most of Dupree's co-workers do not realize that she is black. When one of the people in her office figures this out, it causes a moment of controversy but Dupree continues working. In other words, it doesn't ruin her life or change the office environment. The passing story is in fact not the main narrative line of the film. The main narrative revolves around Dupree being charged with fixing a film in production difficulties that the studio hoped would be a box office success. The film in question is a musical with a white blond female star. The problem is that she is not a good singer and several of the numbers are a disaster.

Illusions refers to the actual practice in Hollywood of bringing in professional singers to dub in better voices. In this case, Dupree calls in a young black female singer named Esther Jeeter (Rosanne Katon). Dupree is kind and respectful toward Jeeter, who makes it clear both that this isn't always the case when she works in Hollywood and that she won't give away Dupree's identity. Depree's intent is not to hide her identity as much as it is to change things within Hollywood.

The heart of the film lies in the session on the soundstage where they work to dub in Jeeter's voice to the already filmed scene. Jeeter remarks that she is usually called in first to lay down the voice track, and then the actresses lip sync to her voice. In this way, Julie Dash highlights the practice of Hollywood to rely on black female talent while at the same time erasing them.[44] Dash then films Jeeter singing on one side of the screen and the film playing on the other side of the screen. Dash moves between the two images and frames them together in stunningly beautiful compositions. At times, Dupree is also in the shot. She is standing behind the glass in the sound studio and is thereby incorporated into the multilayers of cinematic meaning being created. Jeeter's passion is evident as she beautifully sings the song, which breathes life into the musical that was previously garbled.

In this way, Dash points out that the white woman as sexual object exists as an image in relation to black women. In many cases like this one, Hollywood actually builds the image of the white woman as sexual object through the bodies and voices of black women that it subsequently erases. The intersection of race and gender here reveal the way that black female subjects play an integral role and then find themselves cast aside to create white female objects. In making this point, the film creates a questioning stance toward the impact of Hollywood images. In analyzing this scene, Valerie Smith explains, "the identity of the idealized white female subject relies upon rendering invisible her dependency on the labor and identities of black women."[45] In other words, Dash points out that both women are being employed by patriarchy to shore up the fantasies about the white female object.

This revelation happens through the way Dash frames the female body in relation to her surroundings. She shows the relationship between the framed white woman who lacks talent and the off screen black woman who provides the talent but cannot exist within the Hollywood frame. Dash employs her own frame to emphasize the relationship between the women and their relationship to the cinematic frame. Dash's film suggests that Hollywood's frame keeps black and white women apart, and by doing so, it creates a conflicting relationship between them that produces the white female sexual object. This remains an essential critique of Hollywood while suggesting that bringing black and white women together on screen as equals would have a powerful effect on this system.

Illusions creates a highly engaged spectator who enjoys the emotional arcs of Dupree and of Jeeter, the stunning visual compositions, and also the provocative points about the way race and gender work in Hollywood. Dash continues to investigate these topics in her feature length film *Daughters of the Dust*.[46] This film is about the Peazant family, who represents three generations of Gullah women and men. Gullah culture brings together traditions from many different African tribes, ethnic groups, and countries. The Gullah culture was formed when the people brought to the United States as slaves combined their different traditions, as well as the traditions of the white plantation owners (such as Christianity). Dash highlights the unique Gullah culture through dance, food, dialect, and stories told about the past that has guided present day traditions. Cinematically she links this heritage to the family's questions and debates about whether they should move north.

Daughters of the Dust, however, is not as self-reflexive about filmmaking itself since it is a period piece. The film depicts the story of a family on St. Simons Island, Georgia in 1902. The story revolves around the Peazant family's decision to move north off the island in order to find more work and opportunity. Here, Dash presents many different black women and men as they remember the past, navigate the family discord about the approaching move, and think toward the future.

Catherine Cucinella and Renée R. Curry argue that this is a film about a black family's exile within their own country, a story metaphorically about the black experience in the United States. Through a feminist post-colonial reading of the film, they investigate the way that Dash ruptures the mainstream one-note depiction of black femininity with a plethora of black female characters debating their families past and future. They explain: "Dash's exact point is to portray black women in cinema as multifaceted and to portray family as significant but not unidimensional or fixed. Thus, Dash's film dismantles our understanding of an essential and monolithic black woman."[47] The film is decidedly female centered concentrating on the women's individual choices as well as the family relationships between grandmothers, mothers, daughters, outcasts, young women, older women, and women struggling to define themselves. The story stays close to several of the characters but is also about the relationships between all the characters. Hollywood often concentrates on just two or three main characters; Dash, however, branches out to depict a much larger group of central characters' emotional ties to each other and the land they live on. In this way, Dash dramatically changes the mainstream tropes of character development and the visual investigations into women's bodies.

As in *Illusions*, Dash juxtaposes different framings of the female subject next to each other in order to engage the viewer in the meaning that their juxtaposition brings out. Dash interweaves past, present, and future often in one frame, presenting within this frame a story about women collaborating, disagreeing, and supporting each other in making their decisions. Dash often frames the women in striking compositions among the huge trees of the island and on the desolate beaches. Her compositions link and separate their bodies in frames in which the negative space works as much as the positive space in creating a vibrant engagement between the subjects and their surroundings. Dash's frames present the intersection between femaleness and blackness as a vibrant point of subjectivity—one that holds on to antagonism rather than melting into uniformity and complementarity.

Female filmmakers in Hollywood

The fact that Dash and Campion are not making films within Hollywood is part of the reason that their films explore alternative visions of women. Female filmmakers attempting to work within Hollywood have found that when they do manage to get a film funded, they often have to make many changes to their own vision. Male filmmakers entering Hollywood also have to bend to the mainstream expectations of studios that are unwilling to take chances on films that they expect to make money on. Many male filmmakers also cannot experiment or investigate their vision through non-mainstream choices. In other words, they generally have to stay within conventional story modes, propose films within popular genres, mostly employ continuity editing, and cast recognizable actors. They also have to stay away from topics that are too controversial or present controversial topics in acceptable ways. For female filmmakers, however, the types of compromises are greater since most of the prevailing practices have the male at the center.

But even mainstream female filmmakers within Hollywood find that their everyday choices challenge the patriarchal structure of the film industry. One area that female filmmakers have had a little bit more acceptance in is the romance comedy, a genre aimed particularly at a female audience. While this has many ideological implications itself, it has been one of the few genres that female filmmakers have had a little bit of an easier time being employed within. Amy Heckerling is one of the few female directors who has had a long career within Hollywood. Her films are often comedies that have male and female characters that are fairly equal, and the films often depict romance between these equals.

Ranging from *Fast Times at Ridgemont High* (1982) to *Clueless* (1995) to *Loser* (2000), Heckerling's films feature women's points of view even in areas where women do not typically find themselves, such as low comedy. Heckerling struggled to get the studios she worked with to support her choices and see the potential in her films. But she was successful at keeping her films within budget, and audiences loved her comedy. Even still, she says: "I see male directors who can do one bad movie and then a second bad movie and then a third before they finally succeed. And then they are hot directors. I haven't seen a woman do that yet. I always feel that I can't stop, because they'll forget me if I do."[48] Heckerling here suggests that the freedom to fail is as important a freedom as any other.

The production history of Amy Heckerling's iconic teen genre comedy *Fast Times at Ridgemont High* provides a good example. *Fast Times at Ridgemont High* is a raunchy teen comedy. Heckerling's choices at every step often chafed against the male oriented studio expectations. For example, she had to change one of the sex scenes to suit the studio's idea of femininity and masculinity. Before the sex scene, teen Stacy Hamilton (Jennifer Jason Leigh) pursues Mike Damone (Robert Romanus). Mike acts as if he has already had the sexual experiences that other high school students haven't yet had. When Stacy seduces Mike, she stands before him and takes off all her clothes. He does the same. Heckerling meant this image to show both the desire and vulnerability of both young people, but the studio disliked it. The scene would make several points clear. It would reveal that Mike is in fact as inexperienced as Stacy, despite his presentation of himself as experienced. It would also reveal that female and male early sexual experiences can both be equally awkward. The scene would thus emphasize the equality between the experiences of this young man and woman. Both vulnerable and unsure, the symbolism of their nakedness would belie the know-it-all machismo of Mike's behavior in the rest of the film and would bolster the confidence of Stacy putting them on equal footing right before they have sex. Heckerling shot the scene in this way, but the studio felt that this was far too risqué. It demanded that the shots of Mike naked be cut out but that the shots of the naked young woman could remain. This completely changes the scene from two young people equally vulnerable to the woman's body as object of the male look with no possibility for equality. Cutting these key shots from the scene drastically shifted the scene from its potential feminist commentary on the equality of vulnerability in early sexual experiences to a much different scene in which a young woman is objectified and unequal.

Heckerling's experiences are not uncommon for female directors attempting to work within Hollywood. Even the most celebrated and successful women directors in Hollywood confront the difficulties of ideological biases. Female filmmakers are not pure or wholly radical. But throughout the history of film, in varied ways, they have shown the female body without making it into an object. They have highlighted the sexuality of the female subject. They have highlighted the women as the subject of her own story, of history, of the future through narrative centrality and the woman's relation to the world. They have investigated the strength of the female body in many different situations. They have revealed the way patriarchy puts women in positions of subservience even when they are being exalted as a star or worshipped as a sexual icon. They have formally shown women looking at men, other women, and the world around them. They have brought out the complexity of women's failures as much as their successes.

French feminist filmmaker Catherine Breillat, for example, often depicts women in ways that have never been seen on film. She may depict female desire, but she shows it going in unexpected directions. About making films with central women characters she says: "Women are not simple human beings.... A great tenderness and weakness often coexist in women, who are emotional, confused, and fragile. At the same time, they are capable of tremendous violence and aggression in their relationships, in their life in general, and their love life as well, and that includes physical and romantic relationships. Men cannot portray women like that, so it's fairly new to see that in a film."[49] One way to understand Breillat's point here is that spectators should be able to see depictions of women that are not idealized one way or another but representative of the full range of complexities of identity and desire. Engaging the films that women have made allows us to see other possibilities and allows us to glimpse identity as such rather than idealized as a fetishized part. Again, these are not always going to be a panacea, but when there are so few female voices, as there are now in filmmaking, it's very difficult to even know what the other possibilities are.

Throughout its history, feminist film theory has worked to reveal how cinema presents women and to showcase female directors who have made films that reveal the potential for cinema to embrace female desire and not only confine women to patriarchal fantasy. Female fantasy may be no less forgiving, but we can't know until we see it. For the feminist film theorist, thinking about the contradiction of identity allows for a comprehensive understanding of just how the body is being employed ideologically. Through considering the many modes of a spectator's engagement (where the film engages the spectator's desire, fear, anxiety, and so on), the way the female body is positioned in the frame, and the contribution of female filmmakers, the feminist film theorist sheds light on the current representations of women and reveals the fissures within which change may begin to reshape the ideological landscape.

Notes

1   Both essays have since received heavy criticism. Even within
    his own work, Lacan does not often mention the mirror stage,
    but for cinema theorists in the 1970s, it became an essential
    concept, one that contemporary psychoanalytic theorists have
    worked hard to debunk or explain differently.

2   Althusser's idea of ideology is fairly dogmatic. He doesn't
    envision ideology as flexible or interactive with individual
    desire. Instead, he envisions ideology as simply a controlling
    mechanism of society. Even still, his conception of ideology
    allowed subsequent theorists to begin to identify ideology
    in ways they hadn't before even if such theorists, like
    Slavoj Žižek, would take ideology in a much more complex
    direction.

3   Jean-Louis Baudry, "Ideological Effects of the Basic
    Cinematographic Apparatus," trans. Alan Williams, *Film
    Quarterly* 28.2 (1974–1975): 46.

4   Simone de Beauvoir, *The Second Sex*, trans. Constance Borde
    and Sheila Malovany-Chevallier (New York: Alfred A. Knopf,
    2010), 159.

5   Laura Mulvey, "Visual Pleasure and Narrative Cinema," *Screen*
    16.3 (1975): 6–18.

6   Stephen Heath and Peter Wollen also analyzed the impact
    of these structures on the audience through the lens of
    psychoanalysis, Marxism, and semiotics. See Stephen Heath,
    Questions of Cinema (Bloomington, IN: Indiana University
    Press, 1981) and Peter Wollen, *Signs and Meaning in the
    Cinema* (Bloomington, IN: Indiana University Press, 1972).

7   See Claire Johnston, "Women's Cinema as Counter-Cinema,"
    Notes on Women's Cinema (London: Society for Education in
    Film and Television, 1973).

8   Mulvey, "Visual Pleasure and Narrative Cinema," 8.

9   Alice Walker, in her book *In Search of Our Mother's Gardens:
    Womanist Prose*, proposed employing the term womanist
    instead of black feminist theory. She felt feminism could not be
    sufficiently stripped of its racist past and believed that this new
    term was both more independent and more inclusive than black
    feminism. Womanism has been taken up both as an activist

and theoretical term but it has not replaced black feminism completely. In many ways, the term itself also challenges the concept of identification as it calls for a more expansive understanding of identity. See Alice Walker, *In Search of Our Mothers' Gardens: Womanist Prose* (San Diego, CA: Harcourt Brace Jovanovich, 1983).

10   See Kimberle Crenshaw, "Mapping the Margins: Intersectionality, Identity Politics, and Violence Against Women of Color," *Stanford Law Review* 43.6 (1991): 1241–1299.

11   bell hooks, "The Oppositional Gaze: Black Female Spectators," *Black Looks: Race and Representation* (Boston, MA: South End Press, 1992): 116.

12   Theorists writing on film and television began to incorporate these ideas into their textual analysis in the 1990s and 2000s. Valerie Smith, for example, looked back to past films to reconsider their impact in terms of how race and gender intersected and then compared them to contemporary independent films that saw that same intersection in a different way. Her essay, "Class and Gender in Narratives of Passing," considers John Stahl's *Imitation of Life* (1934) and compares it to Julie Dash's *Illusions* (1982) and Charles Lane's *True Identity* (1991). She concludes: "The conditions of passing narratives are, however, productive sites for considering how the intersectionality of race, class, and gender ideologies are constituted and denied; not only do bodies that pass function as markers of sexual and racial transgression, but they signal as well the inescapable class implications of crossing these boundaries." Valerie Smith, "Class and Gender in Narratives of Passing," in *Not Just Race, Not Just Gender: Black Feminist Readings* (New York: Routledge, 1998), 60. Smith's analyses reveal that being aware of the intersections of identity allow filmmakers to explore these sites in new ways and allows scholars to see a fuller picture of how ideology functions as well as where strains of resistance might occur.

13   Patricia White, *Uninvited: Classical Hollywood Cinema and Lesbian Representability* (Bloomington, IN: Indiana University Press, 1999), xvii.

14   In a section entitled, "The Trauma of Joan Copjec," Todd McGowan describes in detail Copjec's relationship to Screen

theory. He says: "In her analysis of Screen theory, Copjec identifies the manifestation of its avoidance of the real—a preoccupation with power at the expense of desire." Todd McGowan, *Psychoanalytic Film Theory and The Rules of the Game* (New York: Bloomsbury, 2015), 65. McGowan asserts that Copjec's ideas so thoroughly undermined the tenets of Screen theory that they could not even acknowledge her points, and it wouldn't be until twenty years later that scholars began to take up her arguments.

15 Joan Copjec, *Read My Desire: Lacan Against the Historicists* (Cambridge, MA: MIT Press, 1994), 14.

16 Beauvoir, *The Second Sex*, 41.

17 Molly Haskell, *From Reverence to Rape: The Treatment of Women in the Movies* (New York: Holt, Rinehart and Winston, 1974), 1.

18 Yvonne Tasker, *Working Girls: Gender and Sexuality in Popular Cinema* (London: Routledge, 1998), 3.

19 E. Ann Kaplan, "The Case of the Missing Mother: Maternal Issues in Video's Stella Dallas," *Feminism & Film* (Oxford: Oxford University Press, 2000), 476.

20 Kathleen R. Karlyn, *Unruly Girls, Unrepentant Mothers: Redefining Feminism on Screen* (Austin, TX: University of Texas Press, 2011), 4.

21 Carol Clover's *Men, Women, and Chain Saws* was another important contribution to feminist film theory that centered on the horror genre. It had an impact both because of its challenge to Mulvey's theory of the male gaze and also for its investigation into the kind of roles that women play in horror films. For example, Clover makes the point that young women who are sexualized in horror films most often die while nonsexualized young women have a good chance of survival; the nonsexualized woman's main task is simply to survive the constant onslaught of male monsters. Clover's "final girl" was a new development in the 1970s in horror film that both spoke to emerging feminism (a young woman who bests the monster) but undermined it at the same time (the young woman was usually a virginal blond white ideal beauty). See Carol Clover, *Men, Women, and Chain Saws: Gender in the Modern Horror Film* (Princeton, NJ: Princeton University Press, 1992).

22 Creed does list repeated character types as well. She says: "The female monster, or monstrous feminine, wears many faces: the amoral primeval mother (*Aliens*, 1986); vampire (*The Hunger*, 1983); witch (*Carrie*, 1976); woman as monstrous womb (*The Brood*, 1979); woman as bleeding wound (*Dressed to Kill*, 1980); woman as possessed body (*Exorcist*, 1973); the castrating mother (*Psycho*, 1960); woman as beautiful but deadly killer (*Basic Instinct*, 1992); aged psychopath (*Whatever Happened to Baby Jane?*, 1962); the monstrous girl-boy (*A Reflection of Fear*, 1973); woman as non-human animal (*Cat People*, 1942); woman as life-in-death (*Life force*, 1985); woman as deadly *femme castratrice* (*I Spit On Your Grave*, 1978)." Barbara Creed, *The Monstrous-Feminine: Film, Feminism, Psychoanalysis* (New York: Routledge, 1993), 1.

23 Creed, *The Monstrous Feminine*, 19–20.

24 Kaja Silverman, *Male Subjectivity at the Margins* (New York: Routledge, 1992), 2.

25 In contrast to Silverman, Susan Jeffords's *Hard Bodies* concentrates on the biopolitical representations of the male action star from the Reagan era. Jeffords argues that the ultra-masculine big-muscled bodies of the Reagan-era blockbuster (such as Rambo and Robocop) presented a body whose unending strength and courage could heal the broken national spirit from Vietnam. As she explains: "The depiction of the indefatigable, muscular, and invincible masculine body became the linchpin of the Reagan imaginary; this hardened male form became the emblem not only for the Reagan presidency but for its ideologies and economics as well." Susan Jeffords, *Hard Bodies: Hollywood Masculinity in the Reagan Era* (New Brunswick, NJ: Rutgers University Press, 1993), 25. Here, though not framing it within Michel Foucault's terms, Jeffords identifies a biopolitical trend in representing the male body by showing the way ideology works to reduce a character and even a nation to the body itself. More specifically, the nation becomes a body that cannot be killed. The indefatigable muscular body in these films represents survival above all else.

26 Silverman, *Male Subjectivity at the Margins*, 270.

27 Hyon Joo Yoo, *Cinema at the Crossroads: Nation and the Subject in East Asian Cinema* (New York: Lexington Books, 2012), 99.

28 Found on the *Bitch Media* website under the "About Our Name" section. Accessed March 1, 2015 http://bitchmagazine. org/about-us.

29 In an article by cofounder of *Bitch* magazine, Lisa Jervis in 2004 argues that the third wave is over. She suggests that the usefulness of the terms has ended because it now is most often used to discuss oppositions between second and third wave feminism. She explains that often the two waves are seen as monolithic and not relatable. She says: "The movement's two current generations have come to be painted as internally monolithic, but they are each as diverse philosophically as feminism itself—they have to be; they *are* feminism itself." Lisa Jervis, "The End of Feminism's Third Wave," *Ms. Magazine* 14.4 (Winter 2004): 58. Accessed February 17, 2015 http:// www.msmagazine.com/winter2004/thirdwave.asp. Jervis calls for recognizing that the generational divide is an illusion and that feminists should continue to disagree and thrive from internal debate. She argues that we need to move beyond the inaccurate idea that the second and third waves are at war. She purposely borrows a phrase from bell hooks here arguing that all feminists want "gender justice." Perhaps this is an important attitude as we move forward. What would "gender justice" look like framed on the large or small screen?

30 The documentary *This Film Is Not Yet Rated* (2006) has a perfect example of this. The filmmaker interviews several directors about their experiences with the ratings board. Director Kimberly Pierce tells of trying to get the board not to give her film *Boys Don't Cry* (1999) an NC-17 rating. The board told her that the scene in which one of her characters has an orgasm goes on too long. Pierce points out that the films of that year had a tremendous amount of violence in them but that the ratings board was more upset about a scene in her film in which a woman experienced pleasure. Pierce notes the ridiculousness of this but suggests that it reveals how actual female pleasure (not the patriarchal fantasy of it) terrifies male dominated cinema.

31 Susan Faludi, *The Terror Dream: Fear and Fantasy in Post-9/11 America* (New York: Metropolitan Books, 2007), 14.

32 In his speech, Moore said: "I have invited my fellow documentary nominees on the stage with us, and we would

like to—they're here in solidarity with me because we like nonfiction. We like nonfiction and we live in fictitious times. We live in the time where we have fictitious election results that elect a fictitious president. We live in a time where we have a man sending us to war for fictitious reasons. Whether it's the fiction of duct tape or fiction of orange alerts we are against this war, Mr. Bush."

33 Only three black actresses have been nominated since Berry's win: Gabourey Sidible for *Precious* (2009), Viola Davis for *The Help* (2011), and Quvenzhané Wallis for *Beasts of the Southern Wild* (2012).

34 Cara Buckley, "Unashamedly Maturing into Her Role: Patricia Arquette, Born for *Boyhood*," *New York Times* (Jan 4, 2015: AR): 18(L). Accessed February 17, 2015 http://www.nytimes. com/2015/01/04/movies/patricia-arquette-born-for-boyhood. html.

35 Sasha Bronner and Emma Gray, "Patricia Arquette Causes Controversy Telling 'Gay People and People of Color' to Fight for Women's Rights," *The Huffington Post* (February 23, 2015). Accessed March 1, 2015 http://www.huffingtonpost. com/2015/02/23/patricia-arquette-controversy-people-of-color-gay-people_n_6734076.html.

36 For a lengthy discussion of the history of violent women on screen, see Hilary Neroni, *The Violent Woman: Femininity, Narrative, and Violence in Contemporary American Cinema* (Albany, NY: State University of New York Press, 2005).

37 See Laura Mulvey, *Visual and Other Pleasures* (Bloomington, IN: Indiana University Press, 1989); Valerie Smith, "Reading the Intersection of Race and Gender in Narratives of Passing," *Diacritics* 24.2/3 (Summer–Autumn, 1994): 43–57; Christina Lane, *Feminist Hollywood: From Born in Flames to Point Break* (Detroit, MI: Wayne State University Press, 2000). See also Anneke Smelik, *And the Mirror Cracked: Feminist Cinema and Film Theory* (New York: Palgrave, 2001), and Geetha Ramanathan, *Feminist Auteurs: Reading Women's Film* (London: Wallflower, 2006).

38 Peter Wollen, "The Auteur Theory," in *Film Theory and Criticism*, eds Leo Braudy and Marshall Cohen (New York: Oxford University Press, 1999), 529.

39 Martha M. Lauzen, "The Celluloid Ceiling: Behind-the-Scenes Employment of Women in the Top 250 Films of 2014." Accessed February 17, 2015 http://womenintvfilm.sdsu.edu/files/2014_Celluloid_Ceiling_Report.pdf, page 1. The Celluloid Ceiling is the longest-running study of the behind the scenes employment in film. The annual study is sponsored by the Center for the Study of Women in Television and Film, San Diego State University.

40 Martha M. Lauzen, "It's a Man's (Celluloid) World: On-Screen Representations of Female Characters in the Top 100 Films of 2014," page 1. Accessed February 17, 2015 http://womenintvfilm.sdsu.edu/files/2014_Its_a_Mans_World_Report.pdf.

41 For a more in depth investigation of this idea see Hilary Neroni, "Following the Impossible Road to Female Passion: Psychoanalysis, the Mundane, and the Films of Jane Campion," *Discourse* 34 (2012): 290–310.

42 Hilary Radner, "'In extremis:' Jane Campion and the Woman's Film," in *Jane Campion: Cinema, Nation, Identity*, eds Hilary Radner, Alistair Fox, and Irène Bessière, (Detroit, MI: Wayne State University Press, 2009), 6.

43 Quoted in Liz Constable, "Unbecoming Sexual Desires for Women Becoming Sexual Subjects: Simone de Beauvoir (1949) and Catherine Breillat (1999)," *MLN* 119.4 (2004): 672.

44 Muriel Smith, for example, was the uncredited ghost singer for April Olrich who played Dolores in Michael Powell's and Emeric Pressburger's *The Battle of The River Plate* (1956), and Smith also was the uncredited ghost singer for Zsa Zsa Gabor in John Houston's *Moulin Rouge* (1953).

45 Valerie Smith, "Reading the Intersection of Race and Gender in Narratives of Passing," *Diacritics* 24.2/3 (1994): 52.

46 Julie Dash tried to get funding for *Daughters of the Dust* from Hollywood, but the studios she approached turned her down. She ended up turning to PBS *The American Playhouse* for funding. Financing a film outside of the studio system is often the only way for female filmmakers in the United States to fund their films.

47 Catherine Cucinella and Renée R. Curry, "Exiled at Home: *Daughters of the Dust* and the Many Post-Colonial Conditions," *MELUS* 26.4 (2001): 201.

48 Quoted in Barbara Quart, *Women Directors: The Emergence of a New Cinema* (New York: Praeger, 1988), 75.
49 Quoted in Robert Sklar and Catherine Breillat, "A Woman's Vision of Shame and Desire: An Interview with Catherine Breillat," *Cinéaste* 25.1 (1999): 24.

CHAPTER TWO

Feminism and
Cléo from 5 to 7

The roles of women

Released in 1962, Agnès Varda's *Cléo de 5 à 7* (*Cléo from 5 to 7*) appeared before the majority of the developments of feminist theory that I've discussed in the previous chapter. As we will see in the following filmic analysis, however, the film remarkably addresses many of the issues still being debated today. The practice of feminist film theory can take many forms, as is evident in the plethora of feminist ideas and approaches already discussed. The following feminist filmic analysis, however, will concentrate specifically on the key analytical approaches developed in the previous chapter, namely analyzing the framing of the female body, the way spectator engagement is created, and the female auteur. Varda is a female auteur whose films dwell on the contradictions of ideal female beauty, expectations of women, and social definitions of women. In this way, her films not only are an excellent example of feminist filmmaking but they also mirror the investigations of feminism itself as they express in their aesthetics the contradictory roles that women are caught between. The exploration of these contradictions is, in Varda's cinema, the central feminist political project.

Varda's films work to engage the spectator to think through the questions that the films raise from the starting point of these antagonisms that women face within the definition of femininity. In other words, this cinema presents its own contradictory relations (between objects in the frame, between genres within one film, between surrealism and realism) in order to highlight the tenuous place of women in society.

One of the exciting aspects of filmic analysis is that for as much as the theorist brings thoughts and ideas to the text, the text also speaks to and broadens those ideas or challenges them. No theory escapes from a textual analysis unscathed. In addition, one of the key aspects to filmic analysis is linking the text to its historical and cultural moment, which allows further understanding of the film itself and provides a moment for current theory to intersect with past artistic expressions. In this way, feminist film theory works to bring past experiences of women, present concerns, and future goals together with the feminist insights that have come out of these moments especially as they might engage a single film or a group of films, which allows us to see the conflicts and contradictions underlying these expressions. "Engage" is a key word here because it indicates an interaction between the film and theory rather than simply an imposition of the theoretical idea. Engagement strengthens and advances the theoretical investigation.

The first gesture of feminist film theory here is to choose *Cléo from 5 to 7* as the film of study and by extension Agnès Varda. Feminist theory works to tackle the experience and philosophical questions of femaleness and femininity as they are located in society. The questions that feminist theory asks are often born out of historical moments of inequality for women as well as the way women are caught between contradictory ideals in society. Thus, part of the project of feminist theory is to theorize the position of people who, though they make up half the population, are often erased from history, politics, and culture.

When feminism acknowledges moments in which women are purposely unacknowledged or barred from participating in an aspect of society, it is also laying bare the very structure of patriarchy. Feminists thus point out that if women are relegated to certain roles in society, this implies that men are not immune to corresponding roles. Men are similarly caught in this trap of patriarchy, and even though they seem to benefit from it, they also lose the freedom to stray too far from what patriarchy expects from them. Thus, many men identify themselves as feminists and engage in feminist theory when they analyze films or culture. Male feminists want women to have equality and adopt the feminist mantra from this concern, but they also recognize the limits that patriarchy puts on masculinity itself.

Nonetheless, even with all the feminist film theory being performed by men and women, it is still rarer for female directors or the films that they make to be written on or taught in classrooms. Alfred Hitchcock, John Ford, Akira Kurasawa, and Jean Luc Godard, for example, have had many books written about them and often appear on syllabi. This is why feminist film theory must concern itself with the disproportionate number of female filmmakers who gain scholarly consideration. Even the most famous female auteurs, such as Jane Campion, Katherine Bigelow, Julie Dash, and others, still rarely receive scholarly or pedagogical attention. It is still a feminist act to choose to study and write on a female directed film.[1]

This does not mean that female directed films are by any means ideologically pure. It just means that their voices are still often unheard so that we don't even have an opportunity to grapple with them, agree with them, or challenge them. Illuminating female-directed films continues to be just one aspect of feminist film theory, which can just as easily analyze any kind of film for its feminist or patriarchal ideas and the way that women are forging their identities in the midst of the contradictory ideals within the social order. Here, however, I will be concentrating on Agnès Varda and her film *Cléo from 5 to 7*.

Agnes Varda was born in 1928 in Brussels, Belgium, but moved to France at an early age and has spent the rest of her life in France. For this reason, despite her birthplace, she sees herself as a French filmmaker, and this is how critics conceive of her as well. She began as a photographer, and her first serious artistic position was with the Théâtre National Populaire. As a photographer at this vibrant important theater, Varda worked with actors and staged photos for plays and advertising. Her approach was to make photos that were performative and creative rather than just documentary in nature. This early experience, along with her background in art history, had a formative effect on her approach to film. She had not actually seen many films when she made her first film, but her involvement in aesthetics and composition had already been significant. Over the course of her career, she has made more than twenty feature films and just as many short films, as well as several made for television films. Her feature films have been both fiction and documentary, as have her shorts.

Varda's relationship to feminism

Varda has been a politically concerned person all her life. She has often discussed her passion for equality for all people in interviews. At times, she articulated her feminist views more overtly—such as when she publicly signed a protest against anti-abortion laws—but other times these views were just part of her own worldview that fueled her creative choices. Putting women at the center of her narrative films and her documentary investigations was an obvious choice for her because it expressed her own interests and desires to explore a woman's adventures and experiences. And yet, in the late 1950s and throughout the 1960s and 1970s, this was a radical choice that had political ramifications, since the majority of the films produced during that period had male protagonists and expressed a patriarchal worldview. Wanting to reach the largest audience possible, however, Varda purposely made her main characters more apolitical and likable to the mainstream even while infusing the form of the film with flourishes that asked the spectator to question how this character's identity was formed. Even though she made these choices, her films were still far from mainstream, and this made it difficult for her to secure funding. She did at one point make her way to Hollywood, but her feminism and artistic sensibility (one of experimentation with a focus on contradiction) made her an unlikely match for a Hollywood studio. The opportunity came about because of her husband, who was also a filmmaker.

Varda met her husband Jacques Demy in the early 1960s, and they had two children. While they were both filmmakers, their films were very different: he made musicals, and she made more experimental fiction and documentary films. Demy received a contract for a film from Columbia Pictures and as a result, Demy and Varda went to California for three years. While there, Varda tried to find funding for films from studios. As Alison Smith explains: "Varda herself never secured a major studio deal, despite a number of efforts and near misses; the disappointment was probably mitigated by the relative liberty that she had in her work."[2] Some feel that it was during this time in California, however, that she had more explicit contact with radical US feminism, which made her own work more explicitly political. Her work that she did in California, in fact, was some of the most explicitly political work that she had done to date. For example, she did a documentary short on the Black Panthers (*Black Panthers*, 1968), another on the Vietnam War (*Loin de Vietnam*, 1967), and a short film critical of the fascist regime in Greece (*Nausicaa*, 1970). Varda herself contradicts the idea that California politicized her in her response to an interviewer who suggested that her relationship to feminism changed in the 1970s. Varda says: "I've been a feminist since I was nineteen years old, fighting for serious rights, for the same wages, for contraception. I started early, early, really."[3] In this same interview, she also comments that she never met a US female director who wanted to talk about filmmaking in the way that she was interested in talking about it and in the way that she was able to talk about it with European female filmmakers (such as Margarethe von Trotta or Chantal Akerman).

This is an important point because it suggests that Varda was interested in how to express ideas about women on the level of form and not as interested in story or overt political activism. In this way, Varda's feminism seemed different from a feminism based in story alone or one that relied heavily on dialogue while relying on a more conventional visual address. Varda's approach meant that it was more difficult to receive funding, even in France where she was well known. In the same interview cited above, Varda explains that she had to fight for the money for every film that she made. And when she couldn't find the money, she says: "I make shorts sometimes just to keep alive in my own research."[4] Varda's commitment to her own vision and the life she set up for herself in France allowed for her to make decisions about the films she would make.[5]

Varda's personal and filmic life was certainly influenced by her feminism. Varda's artistic and political ideas come together in her own unique way—one that is experimental and focuses on the contradictions women face in their existence. Though much celebrated now, Varda was most often not included in a central way in the general history of French cinema.[6] Feminist film theorist Cybelle McFadden points out that in order to right these historical wrongs, Varda began writing her own history, especially in *Les Plages d'Agnès* (*The Beaches of Agnès*, 2008), a film about her own life and her films. McFadden explains: "Varda takes the task into her own hands: her curatorial inscription in *Les Plages d'Agnès* claims her place in French cinema, filling in the gaps left by film historians and critics."[7] There is one section in this film in which she specifically addresses her relationship to feminism. In this section, she discusses—through voice-over and documentary footage—signing a protest against anti-abortion laws. She also interweaves snippets of her own film *Sans toit ni loi* (*Vagabond,* 1986) with documentary footage of feminist protests and news of the women who publically signed this protest against anti-abortion laws along with her. In this way, Varda highlights her personal involvement in the feminist movement and suggests that *Vagabond* especially was an expression of her own feminist ideas—an expression of the anger women experience in the face of oppression.

Varda as auteur

The Beaches of Agnès also reviews Varda's long-held theory about her philosophical approach to filmmaking itself and her vision of herself as an auteur. Articulating a philosophy about your own filmmaking is, of course, not necessary for a filmmaker. There are many who make films without spending time reflecting on the process. But Varda views the formulation of her own aesthetic as part of the filmmaking process. She believes that separating the roles of writer, director, and cinematographer doesn't make sense. As the director, she contends, she expresses her ideas for the film through the writing, the shooting, the editing, and the direction of the actors.

While she often wrote her own screenplays, she felt as director she still metaphorically "wrote" the film visually even when she did not actually pen the screenplay. Thus, she coins the term "cinécriture," filmic writing, to describe her approach. She feels that cinécriture better suggests the integrated process of filmmaking that she employs. Clearly, it also positions the director as author of the film—and thus constitutes Varda's own independently developed version of auteur theory. Considering the lack of women in filmmaking at this time, asserting her position as the director whose vision shapes the entire film also asserted her right to make those decisions. Whether for her own benefit or for those she worked with, this theory about filmmaking had feminist ramifications because it allowed her to better understand and assert her role as director in a predominantly male world.

It also allowed her to focus on exploring her ideas on every level, from the image, to sound, to editing and narrative structure. One of the notable aspects of Varda's work throughout her career is her willingness to experiment and follow her desire wherever it may lead. Ideas for Varda find their expression in a wide variety of forms. The form may be the feature length narrative *Cléo from 5 to 7* (1961), the short documentary *Black Panthers*, or a video installation piece *My Shack of Cinema* (1968–2013), which was on display in the Los Angeles County Museum of Art's exhibition "Agnès Varda in Californialand" in 2013. While her choice of format was also tied to the material changes in her own life, her philosophy of seeing film as cinécriture allowed her to consider everything she made as a total expression of her ideas.

To understand Varda as an auteur and to better analyze *Cléo from 5 to 7*, it is imperative to investigate her films before and after she made *Cléo from 5 to 7*. I will do this as I explain some of her stylistic and thematic concerns that express her vision, even though this vision changes over time. Her theory of cinécriture itself reveals her intense interest in the way that form itself can express ideas. These ideas do not have to be specific to the plot but are often broader and philosophical. One stylistic and theoretical interest of Varda—inextricably tied to her feminism—is the power of contradiction to reveal deeper meaning about people and their communities. For Varda, this can be contradictory images, storylines, genres, camera movement, and so on. For example, in her first film *La Pointe Courte* (1955), she combines two different stories that do not necessarily go together. In an interview, she explains that she based the film formally on William Faulkner's *The*

Wild Palms, in which one chapter tells the story of a couple and the other chapter tells the story of two escaped prisoners.[8] The novel moves back and forth between the two storylines, and they never intersect. *La Pointe Courte* also has two stories that run throughout the film, one about a couple whose relationship seems in question and one about the inhabitants in the village where they are staying. The loose link between the stories is that the man is from this village, but other than this tenuous connection, the two story lines do not engage each other. Instead, the engagement happens in the way the viewer experiences these two stories as they alternatingly unfold. When talking about the form of this film, Varda says, "It could be seen as the clash between private life and social life, which can never be joined. It's a contradiction that's inherent in our lives and that I think everyone understands. I tried to express it on film, calmly, abstractly."[9] She does this by showing two different ways of seeing, as she puts it, that embody the two different worlds which exist together but can never come together.

One of the ways she expresses this is by staging and shooting the actors differently in the separate story lines. The storyline about the couple is much more theatrical and stylized. They stand or sit while they talk to each other, and sometimes the film positions them quite unnaturally toward each other as they say their lines. Varda instructed them to say their lines flatly and not to try to put too much emotion into the lines, so the acting also comes off as unnatural. The storyline about the village, however, is shot in a much more documentary-like manner as the camera wanders around the village. Additionally, the actors employ a much more naturalistic style and indeed Varda even employed local townspeople to essentially play themselves. And while it expresses the story, this engaging film also expresses Varda's theories about the inherent clash between private and public life—the contradiction between these two modes of existence.

The spectator generates the meaning of the film that arises from the clashing of these two different story lines and Varda is particularly interested in this engagement. She comments: "I tried to avoid taking the easy way out when you tell a story you explain everything and then its over. I'm more interested in trying to find something that forces me to find a new filmic language that continually sets up new relationships between the person who envisions and creates the film and the person who sees it. I'm always thinking of the viewer."[10] In this way, Varda actively works to create an engagement between the viewer and her films in which the viewer is part of the meaning making process.

Varda's idea of actively engaging the viewer leads to her approach of employing many different styles of filmmaking often within a single film.[11] Or she chooses two styles that normally directors don't use together, as she does in the contrasting storylines in *La Pointe Courte*. She often combines narrative conventions with documentary conventions or with performance art tropes, and the effect is that she confounds genre expectations. She does this with more complexity as she matures as a filmmaker, but even her early films reveal that she does not feel constrained to just one idea of narrative filmmaking—and certainly does not feel constrained to abide by traditions and expectations followed in Hollywood mainstream cinema. But the result is not chaotic films or films that fail to satisfy the viewer. Instead, Varda is able to combine approaches in a way that engages the viewer. In this sense, Varda's approach functions as an example of privileging spectator engagement over identification. Varda is not as interested in the spectator's identifying with a character in a particular way as she is intent on the spectator engaging in actively seeing the links between the contradictions or the mixed styles and shots.

Varda is especially known for her pioneering films in which women take center stage. Simply by placing women at the center of her narratives, she defies the traditional narrative approach. For example, *Cléo from 5 to 7* depicts a popular female singer as she deals with waiting to hear a cancer diagnosis; *Vagabond* depicts the day in a life of a homeless woman before she dies; *Les Glaneurs et la Glaneuse* (*The Gleaners and I*, 2000) stars Varda herself as she investigates whether the practice of gleaning excess from crop harvests still exists in France. And in films such as *La Pointe Courte*, the women constitute a central part of the town and an equal part in the relationship.

Varda's characters challenge traditional depictions and the way Varda frames the female body contributes to this non-patriarchal approach. For example, Varda investigates pregnancy in her film *L'Opéra Mouffe* (*Diary of a Pregnant Woman*, 1958). Instead of depicting a glowing happy pregnant woman, Varda explores the contradictions in pregnancy and even the philosophical questions it might bring up. She shoots the pregnant woman's body naked at times but presents the pregnant body to be analyzed in relationship to the rest of the environment. For example, she includes a shot of a huge pumpkin that the spectator can't help but relate to the pregnant belly. In analyzing this film, film theorist Delphne Bénézet remarks: "Varda's determination to question the corporeal and her desire not to limit herself to stereotyped versions of female subjectivity shows that *L'Opéra Mouffe* is as feminist as De Beauvoir's writing."[12] Clearly mainstream images of women and of pregnant women are also corporeal insofar as their main focus is the female body itself, but Bénézet suggests that Varda's way of depicting the pregnant body puts her work on par with the French feminist philosopher Simone de Beauvoir because it provokes the spectator to think about how that body is treated by and situated in the social order. This is the polar opposite of romanticizing the pregnant body.[13]

Varda's filmmaking style and subject matter, however, do not fit comfortably into a portrait that all feminist activists or theorists might paint of a feminist filmmaker. This is not a contingent fact but a conscious choice on Varda's part. She felt that overt feminist topics or types of characters would reduce the potential number of viewers, and thus she prefers to locate the feminism into the form of her films. By emphasizing spectator engagement through an eclectic style, Varda promotes a thoughtful spectator who would not only be engaged by the beauty of the image and the emotion in the story but also by the feminist associations that the filmmaking style promotes. As a result of this political decision, Varda often confounds feminists and non-feminists alike. She thwarts critical expectations and produces a feminism of form rather than content.

Varda and the French New Wave

Varda was not alone in the creation of an eclectic filmic style in the 1950s and 1960s in France. She was part of an exciting movement of young filmmakers eventually called the French New Wave, which refers to a group of films and filmmakers in France who overthrew existing cinematic traditions. Shooting on the streets with handheld cameras for lower budgets and often with young actors, the French New Wave experimented with new topics and styles. Scholars often say that the French New Wave movement began in 1959 and ended in 1963, but films inflected by the New Wave exist both before and after this period. Influenced by both Italian Neorealism and Hollywood films, the French New Wave brought together realist techniques (such as shooting on location in ambient light) with fictional stories of intrigue, crime, and youthful rebelliousness.

The films often brought together a sense of humor with poignant tragedy. The legend of the formation of the French New Wave is that a handful of young men—specifically, François Truffaut, Jean-Luc Godard, Éric Rohmer, Claude Chabrol, and Jacques Rivette—who didn't know each other began to see each other at a movie house that screened an eclectic variety of Hollywood and international films. They became friends and began to write for a journal called *Cahiers du Cinéma* under the tutelage of film theorist André Bazin.

Within the pages of this journal, they analyzed films, proffered theories about filmmaking (such as the auteur theory), and considered the formal qualities that they valued and disdained in the films they had seen. Eventually, they began to make their own films and these films make up the French New Wave. Except for the films of Jean Renoir and a few others like him, the French New Wave rebelled against French cinema, which consisted largely of historical dramas and sex farces with elaborate spectacular sets along with predictable plotlines. The French New Wave was something wholly different. It brought an experimental attitude to the cinema that would define much of European cinema for years to come. When one hears the legend, the question of Varda's position within it inevitably comes up.

The legend of the formation of the New Wave doesn't include Varda, and yet Varda herself made one of the first French New Wave films. *La Pointe Courte*, made in 1955, has all the features of what would later become the French New Wave. The film was not shown publically until 1957, when many of the stalwarts of the nascent French New Wave were in the audience. This was before any of the five greats of the New Wave had made a feature film of his own. It might be too much to say that Varda herself founded the New Wave and that her film shaped the subsequent debuts of filmmakers like Truffaut and Godard, but it is the case that she merits a place in the legend.

The story of the genesis of the New Wave also excludes Alain Renais and Chris Marker, two other male French filmmakers whose initial work appeared before the most famous French New Wave films. Like Varda, their films resemble the other more famous New Wave films that would follow in their wake. Critics often call Varda, Renais, and Marker the Left Bank filmmakers of the French New Wave. They worked in a similar vein and started a little earlier, but they were not part of the *Cahiers du Cinema* group. Even still, Renais and Marker often receive more attention then Varda in film history, though more recently the accounts have corrected this oversight.

Varda's second feature length fiction film, *Cléo from 5 to 7*, falls directly in the middle of the French New Wave movement both in terms of chronology and in terms of style and theme. Varda's initial exclusion from the legend of the French New Wave and her progression into that history in the last couple decades is indeed a good example of recent attempts to correct film history that ignored female filmmakers. This type of historical reclamation is a project that a diverse group of feminists have been working on since the 1970s. There are stories like Varda's throughout the history of film in which women filmmakers were forgotten simply because of a male-oriented view of that history.

Varda's own experience of the other French New Wave filmmakers was cordial and supportive. They all were very positive about both *La Pointe Courte* and *Cléo from 5 to 7*. But Varda still felt like the odd woman out in that group. She tells about Alain Renais bringing her to meet the *Cahiers* group for the very first time and her feeling marginalized as the only woman there. About that evening, she says, "They quoted thousands of films and suggested all sorts of things to Resnais, they all talked fast, chatted brightly, and sat everywhere including on the bed. I seemed to be there by mistake, feeling small, ignorant and the only woman among the guys from *Cahiers*."[14] After this, however, she did work further with some from this group. For example, Jean-Luc Godard acted in the film within the film in *Cléo from 5 to 7*.

Nonetheless, it's important to recognize that Varda made films in this environment of experimentation and risks in filmmaking. Even though she was not part of the boys club, their thought and films allowed her to do the work she did, just as her own work opened doors for their films. In many ways, they set the stage for each other, but Varda was still often the only woman on the film crew and the only woman filmmaker in the room asking for financing, which put her at a disadvantage. The fact that she was the rare woman in a male-dominated industry shaped Varda's career as a filmmaker. That said, she also carved her own path and made films that expressed her ideas and artistic interests without catering too much to mainstream acceptance or acceptance by the male filmmakers surrounding her.

Nowhere is her unique cinematic vision more fully elaborated than in *Cléo from 5 to 7*. Even though this is just her second fictional feature, all of Varda's formal inventiveness manifests itself in this work. She creates one of the greatest feminist masterpieces in the history of cinema by enacting the contradictions of femininity and forcing the viewer to experience these contradictions without any means of escape. To watch the film properly is to recognize that the contradictions of femininity point us toward those of society—and in this way *Cléo from 5 to 7* enables us to see that feminism is not just a project of female emancipation but an emancipatory project for all of society.

The beautiful trap

Cléo from 5 to 7 opens with a scene that reveals a beautiful and famous singer, Florence "Cléo" Victoire (Corinne Marchand), may have cancer. She spends the rest of the film wandering between the people in her life and the shops, art studios, and streets of Paris as she contemplates how she feels about this news. In her wanderings, she confronts existential crises and many unanswered questions. At times, it is difficult to feel sympathy for this main female character because she is so enamored with her own image and so coddled by her entourage that she seems simply unlikeable. The film does not present Cléo as a feminist hero with whom we should identify—that is not Varda's brand of feminism—but rather uses her to demonstrate the contradictions of femininity. It is with these contradictions that the viewer must engage in order to recognize the film's version of feminism.

The most intense of these moments of contradiction occur when Cléo is the most uncertain about her own identity—specifically, when Cléo is attempting to study her own image in mirrors that she finds throughout her journey. Varda reveals Cléo's image in the mirror as becoming more and more fractured as the film progresses. These interactions with her mirrored image are both the moments of Cléo's greatest pain and anxiety, but they are also the strongest moments of engagement for the spectator with an otherwise unappealing heroine. These moments are also some of the most existential moments in the film as Cléo explicitly wonders who she is and how her beauty relates to her identity. The course of Cléo's travels also formally brings her beauty into contact with other people's expectations and with the social fiber of Paris itself. As a result, the film is a rich text to explore the incongruent contours of female identity through feminist analysis.

Cléo from 5 to 7 is about a woman who seems to enjoy and embody her femininity as object. The film investigates the relationship between her beauty as commodity, her enjoyment of her beauty, her enjoyment of consuming products that signify femininity, and her anxiety over a possible diagnosis of cancer. It is on the level of form, however, that the film suggests the potential meaning that could come out of these relations. As the title suggests, the film is about Cléo's day from 5:00 p.m. to 7:00 p.m. On the one hand, the film's title marks the time of day during which the events in the film take place. On the other hand, the title refers to French slang (a "cinq à sept") that suggests a sexual affair deriving from the time that such affairs usually took place. Despite this possible allusion in the title, Varda's film is not about Cléo having an afternoon sexual liaison but rather about Cléo having a brief but intense affair with the possibility of death. It begins with a tarot reader seeing the death card in her future and the sure diagnosis of cancer, which the tarot reader doesn't tell Cléo but is absolutely clear to the tarot reader herself. The rest of the film is about Cléo's wanderings through the city of Paris and interactions with several friends and colleagues. Each new experience is broken into chapters, as if the film had the structure of a novel.

Cléo's beauty as an anchoring aspect to her identity is announced visually at the beginning of the film but also constantly by Cléo herself. A few scenes later, we discover that Cléo is a well-known singer with several hit singles. Nearly everyone she meets (except the final man she makes friends with) comments that she is beautiful but that she is also a spoiled child (though they don't say this to her face). They all profit off her beauty (her maid, the song writers, her boyfriend) except her friend Dorothée (Dorothée Blanck), who is a model, and the friend she makes at the end of the film, Antoine (Antoine Bourseiller).

Before considering how the film investigates Cléo's beauty, it is worth taking a detour to discuss generally how society commonly thinks about and discusses beauty. When we perceive women as beautiful, we tend to link this beauty to their biology. One of the reasons the idea of female beauty is such a strong ideological idea is that it is tied to the body. One often hears: "she is lucky because she was born beautiful," or "her beauty was a curse to her," and so on. The ideology of female beauty suggests that some lucky women are born beautiful and others are not. What no one proclaims, however, is that female beauty is as much a system of signification as anything else in society. That is, ideal female beauty has its own set of social signifiers or symbols. It functions just like a language. The truth is that most women know this even if they don't articulate it. This is why women obey the customs of their culture with regard to how women should dress, wear their hair, shave, wear make-up, wear jewelry, position their body, and use their voice. As much as society would like us to believe that female beauty is just biological and some women are just lucky, there are a multitude of body and behavior modifications that signify ideal female beauty, and one must adopt these signifiers in order to gain the appellation "beautiful."

These modifications in and of themselves should cancel out the ideological strength of the idea of an inherent female beauty, but this is not the case. For example, consider the role that celebrities play in the ideology of female beauty. A photographer will catch a photo of a female celebrity with no make up on or who is unshaven or who looks heavier than she usually does in films, and magazines will present these photos with headlines about the celebrity's decline or her inability to take care of herself. Rather than undermining the ideological link between beauty and biology, such proclamations work to solidify the average woman's belief in keeping up the rituals of beauty (such as wearing make up, shaving, or dieting).

Certain women's biology may coincidentally match the ideal beauty of their culture and historical moment, but this only serves to strengthen everyone's belief in this ideal beauty and thus strengthen women's devotion to the customs of dress and body modification that women feel they have to perform to look beautiful. Certainly, there are many people in society who overlook or see beyond this ideology. They find people beautiful for a vast number of reasons or they feel themselves to be beautiful even if society has deemed them not to be. But it is clear to anyone who looks through the internet sites, magazine pages, films, television series, and advertising that ideal female beauty is still fully operative in popular culture. It is used to sell products and it is used to influence women's behavior. It also suggests that a woman's worth is dependent on her luck to be beautiful or her devotion to the dress and body modification that signify beauty. Additionally, adhering to ideas of ideal beauty also puts women in the position of being looked at rather than looking.

The recent *Cinderella* (Kenneth Branagh, 2015) provides a contemporary yet traditional example. When Cinderella (Lily James) arrives at the ball in this and most versions, everyone turns to stare at her and is dazzled by her beauty. She walks or floats through the ball and the crowd parts while staring at her, and the prince (Richard Madden) meets her on the dance floor. As they start to dance, she says to him: "They are all looking at you." And he replies: "Oh believe me, it's you they are looking at." Here, Cinderella's symbolic identity is defined completely by how others, and this means everyone in the kingdom, looks at her. And while the Prince might look quite handsome, he is not defined by how they are looking at him, and he clearly takes up the position of the one looking.[15]

Cléo from 5 to 7 ties these questions of beauty, looking, and women's place in culture and popular culture to questions of death, existential crisis, and subjectivity. In doing this, Varda powerfully interrogates how ideologies of beauty shape subjectivity. To do this, she initially presents Cléo as a natural beauty in a way that seems wholly ideological. She is tall, blond, thin, and has a model's face. Varda solidifies this by repeatedly showing people's reactions to her beauty. They turn to stare at her on the street, and people constantly comment on her beauty. She wears flattering stylish dresses and has her hair up in a dramatic fashion. But in various scenes, Varda begins to probe this idea of Cléo's beauty.

Varda calls the most attention to the accoutrements of Cléo's femininity and beauty in a scene at Cléo's apartment. The staged and nearly ridiculous nature of this scene works to counter Cléo's physical beauty, or rather it works to emphasize all that is necessary to create this beauty. This scene stands out as the most fantastical in the film and the one in which Cléo's beauty and her rituals of femininity seem completely staged rather than natural. The provocative aspect to this performance of femininity is that it occurs not in public but in her private home. While it is clear that Cléo performs her femininity in public or at least expects the public to notice her beauty, this scene at her house indicates that she also has to continue performing her femininity when people aren't looking. It is significant that when she comes to a place of self-recognition at the end of the film, she is in a public space—a large park—rather than in a private space like her own home.

By locating Cléo's authentic self-recognition in public and by emphasizing the performance that occurs in private, Varda reverses our typical conceptions of public and private. The private world ceases to be a respite from illusory presentation of one's self and becomes instead the place of a primordial self-deception. The public world, in contrast, functions as the site where one can undergo an encounter that could collapse the performance of female beauty.

In the scene in her apartment, Cléo and her maid, Angèle (Dominique Davray), have returned from their outing (which I discuss later), and they enter Cléo's home. When they enter, we see a large white room and a large black bed. It resembles a stage rather than an apartment. Several scenes occur in the apartment that inform the spectator's understanding of Cléo's relationship to her beauty and her identity. While they are in the apartment, various people visit—Cléo's boyfriend and her songwriters. When the latter visit, Cléo practices singing her new songs with them. During these visits, Angèle cares for all her needs. When Cléo and Angèle first walk in, Cléo kicks off her shoes, and Angèle comes with slippers and helps her take off her dress to reveal a beautiful slip. In these scenes, the maid pampers Cléo like a doll or child, which is a standard way of imagining how beautiful wealthy women are treated. The clothes she wears are extremely feminine. They include a lush housecoat, which is white satin with many layers and feathers around the collar and large sleeves, as well as slippers topped with large flowers. The housecoat acts as one of the main props in the ensuing scenes, providing an interior frame within the shot of her face that signifies femininity. After stretching for two minutes, Cléo goes to lie down on her bed and requests a hot water bottle for her stomach. Angèle brings the bottle, which is in the shape of a kitten. Going along with this kitten-shaped water bottle, there are actual kittens playing in the room and on the bed.

The doorbell rings, and Angèle cautions: "Don't say you're ill. Men hate illness." With this piece of advice, Angèle acts as Cléo's femininity coach. Indeed, Angèle's job relies on Cléo's success as a popular singer and thus on her feminine beauty. As Cléo awaits her visitors, the camera frames her in a sexual way, mimicking how a Hollywood film shoots a starlet. Varda here emphasizes the performance of femininity not only with Cléo's costume but also with camera work and with music. Cléo moves sexily on the bed, picks up a kitten and kisses it, while the white flounces of the housecoat frame Cléo and the kitten. The endless whiteness further emphasizes Cléo's type of beauty. In this shot, she resembles more a model on an advertising set than the star of a French New Wave film. Varda brings together different types of cinema in order to engage the spectator and highlight the contradictions in the creation of beauty. In other words, Varda uses the form—the set, props, camera movements, lighting, and editing—to indicate a predominant trope of female beauty. Rather than highlight this in the dialogue or the plot, Varda employs different filmic styles to engage the viewer in thinking about and questioning how the female must become beautiful.

Varda's positioning of the camera exposes Cléo's concern for constituting herself as beautiful. She keeps the camera on Cléo while Angèle shows her boyfriend in. Cléo settles herself into the bed and picks up a hand mirror to check her face, which indicates her incessant involvement in producing her beauty. She then puts the mirror down and assumes a pouty sexy look while her boyfriend walks up to her. Varda overlays a track of sentimental music that one might find in a popular romantic film, and this reveals to the viewer the clichéd nature of Cléo's actions.

Cléo takes Angèle's advice about the illness and does not reveal to her boyfriend the nature of the problem. Instead, she plays the coquette. When he finds the water bottle and asks if she's sick, she says yes. He tells her: "You're strong. Your beauty is your health." This startling line indicates that her lover openly values beauty above all other aspects of Cléo and even sees it as a magic power giving her the ability to triumph over any ailment. Her boyfriend is a successful businessman who has a lot of money, and he thus functions as the ideological complement to the beautiful woman. But due to the excessive and fantastical presentation of this scene, Varda authors a thoroughgoing critique of both figures in this couple.

The subsequent scenes in the apartment similarly investigate the expectations that others have of Cléo and reveal that everyone considers her through the lens of her attractiveness. These scenes continue in a similar vein by including other performances of femininity. Steven Ungar points out how this occurs during the sampling of songs that she rehearses in the apartment. He says: "As they move through bits and pieces of songs, each successive composition evokes a different female persona—the woman of a thousand faces, the gold digging liar, the flirt—that Cléo seems to sample, much as she had tried on hats."[16] Eventually, however, Cléo is overwhelmed by everyone's expectations of her behavior and she abruptly leaves. With this depiction, Varda underlines the oppressiveness of female beauty.

Before she leaves, Cléo abandons the markers of beauty. She changes to a simple black dress and she pulls her wig off. Underneath, she has blond hair, but it is short, cut to her chin. As she pulls it off, she says: "I wish I could pull my head off as well." This is the first moment that she articulates an adversarial relationship to her own beauty. Angéle offers to come, but Cléo says that she wants to be alone. She does stop to take a necklace and her new hat and put it on along with a shawl, which shows that her new proclamation does not extend to all her accessories of beauty. Yet this scene does mark a turning point in Cléo's ability to see how the markers of beauty that provide social status also erase her subjectivity. She leaves and immediately encounters a mirror.

Mirroring the subject

Mirrors in *Cléo from 5 to 7* serve simultaneously as symbols of femininity and sites of encounter. Cléo cannot begin to overcome her own investment in the ideal of female beauty until she stops looking at herself in mirrors. And yet, her encounters with mirrors also seem to precipitate this emancipation as well. Looking into the mirrors, Cléo finds the ideal beauty that she works hard to attain, but at the same time she also often sees a distortion within that image. The film suggests through the framing of the female body that the distortion is her beauty itself: beauty functions as its own distortion as much as it functions as an ideal.

Cléo endeavors to see herself in the mirror, but in the end she sees only her beauty, which both defines her and obliterates her at the same time. It defines her because it provides symbolic status, economic stability, and male attention. It obliterates her because it is an ideological fantasy that does not include her own subjectivity. This antagonism at the heart of female beauty between symbolic identity and the erasure of subjectivity manifests itself in distortions in the mirror images. There are several scenes throughout the film that involve mirrors, and their appearance follows a logical progression. In other words, each mirror scene moves to a new type of distortion that adds insight into Cléo.

Mirrors play a crucial role in femininity in the contemporary world. Women spend much more time scrutinizing themselves in front of mirrors than men do, as they carefully craft their own image to fit (or possibly challenge) the social conception of ideal beauty. It might appear that the ultimate challenge to ideal beauty would be never to look in a mirror again. While various iterations of feminism (especially in the 1970s) would certainly appreciate this gesture, it might not actually address the underlying issues of beauty and femaleness in our society. This is because the mirror is not simply a mirror of ideology. They are also the site for an encounter with ideological contradictions. Varda focuses on mirrors as a way to precipitate this encounter while at the same time exposing how women are beholden to their mirrored image.

Varda's own relationship to mirrors in her filmmaking suggests that her focus on mirrors was not just a gimmick in this one film but rather part of a lifelong investigation. Mirrors turn up often in Varda's films, and this culminates in *The Beaches of Agnes*. This film is autobiographical, and it begins with Varda on a beach that she visited often as a child. Varda has numerous mirrors of all kinds set up on the beach. The film reveals the crew setting up the mirrors and Varda telling the crew where to put the mirrors in the sand. Varda also shows herself shooting the mirrors with both still and video cameras. She takes abstract shots that often depict one mirror reflecting into another, framed by the sand and water.

In one shot, Varda faces away from the water shooting the beach and the dunes under the gray and windy sky. A well-placed mirror in the lower third of the frame, however, reflects not only the beach but also Varda filming the scene. The image offers a glimpse of Varda's own self-investigation. The mirrors here both act as reflections of real life and as beautiful art objects that abstract the landscape and thereby add something new to the scene. This is, I think, what Varda is after in her attention to the mirror.

The mirror provides a secondary source of reflection in the world, one which both doubles and abstracts from the objects it reflects. In this way, the mirror has some relationship to the movie screen, which also doubles the object that it presents. These images appear as reflections of real life, but they are also distortions of it. Women live in a world of mirrors and screens, which define a certain kind of femininity. Varda's use of the mirror questions the role that the distortion of reality plays in our lives, but her answer to this problem is not a simple rejection of the mirror image. As she sees it, one can only find the truth of one's situation through the doubled distortion of it. The distorting effect of the image must, however, become evident for the truth to manifest itself. Varda shifts and tilts the mirror, or she divides it and cracks it, in order to reflect the everyday in a new way. This allows her to create even more distortion in the mirror image. The mirror tells the truth not when it reflects perfectly what is in front of it but when it creates a revelatory distortion.

The first mirror scene comes at the beginning of the film just after Cléo has received the bad news about her future from the Tarot card reader. She stops at the lobby mirror on her way out and looks at herself. In an interior comment she says to herself: "Don't rush away, pretty butterfly. Ugliness is a kind of death. As long as I'm beautiful, I'm alive and ten times more so than others." (In French she says: "Minute beau papillon : être laide, c'est ça la mort. Tant que je suis belle, je suis vivante et dix fois plus que les autres.")[17] Cléo sees her beauty as vitalizing: it renders her much more alive than others. Clearly this statement, made while looking at herself, indicates her belief in both her own beauty and the power of ideal female beauty. Cléo seeks out mirrors to confirm her beauty or to see if her beauty is dying in the way that she fears her body is. She also equates losing her beauty with death.

Cléo is fully embedded in the ideology that proclaims female beauty as the essence of a woman's identity. In this scene, she asserts her beauty's power to make her superior to others, and she looks to the mirror to deflect the prediction of death. The shot itself, however, makes another kind of commentary. The dark shadow that covers half Cléo's face undermines the confidence of her assertion. It also suggests that this very point of confidence is also the point of Cléo's erasure. Her ideal beauty elides her subjectivity. The structure of the shot challenges the imaginary validation that we want the mirror to provide. Varda shoots this scene in such a way that the mirroring effect goes on to infinity. Cléo's encounter with her own image is repeated again and again into the infinite depth of the mirror because there is a mirror on either side of the hall. Varda films Cléo looking in one mirror, but it reflects the mirror across the hall catching this action thus reduplicating her image over and over. The infinity of the mirror image reveals both its illusoriness and its distorting effect.

This repetition provides an excess of Cléo's image, an excess that turns the scene into a question instead of a reassurance of beauty. The scene is reminiscent of a similar scene of an image of Charles Foster Kane (Orson Welles) endlessly repeated in a mirror when he is aging and alone in his palace in *Citizen Kane* (Orson Welles, 1941). At the moment when he has lost everything he cares about and has given way to his anger and desperation, Welles films Kane as he walks by a mirror opposed by another mirror. The repeated image that results symbolizes the dissolution of Kane's symbolic identity and his inability to feel in control as death looms imminent.

This infinite mirroring sheds light on the repeating image in *Cléo from 5 to 7*. The two differ in that Cléo's infinite mirroring scene comes at the beginning of the film, but it also signals a crisis in her identity and the approach of death. For Cléo, the question of female beauty has a central role in the infinite mirroring in a way that it doesn't for Kane. In patriarchal society, ideal female beauty guarantees symbolic status, a status that signifies life for Cléo but which begins to seem inconsequential in the face of potential death. The repeated image here provides her comments about her vitality with a visual counterpoint that throws her assertions into question. The excess of the mirroring punctuates ideal female beauty with a contradiction that points to its eventual loss.

Mirrors themselves seduce us into believing that we can see subjectivity, that we can see ourselves in the process of seeing. They offer the illusion of unmediated insight into ourselves. But this scene makes clear that there is no such thing as pure seeing: our psychic structure and our social investments always mediate how we look, even when we look straight into a mirror. Through the excessive repetition in the mirror, Varda hints at the fantasy that women engage in when they check on their beauty in the mirror. Rather than encountering just the reality of their image, they instead encounter a thoroughly mediated version of themselves. The ideological fantasy of female beauty shapes what one sees in the mirror. But the key to ideology is that we don't notice it, especially when it is at its strongest. Thus, a woman concerned with seeing ideal beauty in the mirror cannot see the way that her seeing operates through an ideological fantasy. This is what Varda is slowly trying to unpack in *Cléo from 5 to 7*. Varda employs distortions—here in the form of an infinite mirroring—to engage the viewer's investment in the ideological fantasy of ideal beauty.

The distortion reveals that the ideal of female beauty is not hiding a true self waiting to emerge from beneath it. If one could rip the ideological ideal of femininity away, one would not find some more authentic female subject. But this is not particular to femininity; it reflects the nature of subjectivity itself. Subjectivity is neither the symbolic identities we cling to nor the void beneath them but rather the way we are situated between the two. Subjectivity is the failure of the woman to see herself in the ideal of female beauty.

In *Cléo from 5 to 7*, to paraphrase Joan Copjec, the mirrors functions as a screen that reveals femininity to be precarious.[18] Even though the mirror provides a vehicle for an ideological fantasy, it also reveals the split in subjectivity. The distortions of the mirror lead to insight for the viewer but not necessarily for Cléo within the diegesis. Varda's concern is for the viewer to see the disjunction between beauty and subjectivity. At the moment that beauty seems to affirm subjectivity, it erases it. The film exposes this contradiction in order to allow the spectator to grapple with the problem of femininity and beauty.

Another mirror scene follows directly after the one of infinite mirroring. Cléo enters a café to meet her maid Angèle but she can't cheer up because she cannot shake her existential dread. She looks into a mirror at the point where it connects to another mirrored panel, and the seam between the mirrors distorts her face. She asks her maid Angèle if death is written on her face, while the spectator sees the seam dividing her face from itself and thereby disturbing the image of female beauty. Staring at the mirror, Cléo says, "If it is, I'll kill myself." She turns to a mirror to find the image of female beauty that will anchor her, but instead she sees a distortion of her face split in two by the seam of the two panels. It is as if the distortion is death itself interrupting her beauty and, consequently, her identity. But in a few moments, a coffee and attention from the waiters relieves her feeling of dread. After she calms down and they leave the café, Cléo and Angèle walk along the street and discover a hat shop whose window display catches their attention.

When they go into the shop, Cléo immediately brightens up. In this scene, Varda emphasizes another aspect of female beauty operative in most advanced capitalist countries—consumerism. Ideal beauty has an intrinsic connection to the act of consumption. The woman invested in ideal beauty must know how to shop for the proper beauty products (for hair, face, nails, legs, and so on) and proper services in order to maintain her adherence to the ideal. But women's relationship to consumption is dual. On the one hand, companies use women's bodies to sell products. They display the woman's body as a sexual object that the consumer identifies with the purchase of the product. In advertisements that display a woman's body, the body itself becomes the product being sold. But on the other hand, a large percentage of advertising aims at women themselves, trying to convince them to invest themselves in the ideal of female beauty. Advertising attempts to persuade women that the proper commodity will allow them to attain ideal beauty, even though the ideal exists only insofar as no one can attain it.

This message often comes in the form of ideas about the female body: that it should be skinnier, hairless, blemish-free, and wrinkle-free. Advertisements promoting ideal female beauty have been prevalent throughout the history of advertising, and they were certainly in the air when Varda made *Cléo from 5 to 7*. For instance, the tagline for the 1954 ad for Lustre-Crème Shampoo reads, "Lustre-Crème Shampoo Never Dries—it Beautifies." The advertisement suggests that dry dull hair falls short of ideal beauty and that this product will ensure that one's hair doesn't fall short. The advertisement features the celebrity actress Jane Powell, whose blond hair, blue eyes, flawless skin, and perfect make-up constitute the image of ideal beauty that Hollywood put forth in the 1950s. Stars such as Maureen O'Hara, Doris Day, Elizabeth Taylor, and Ava Gardner all appeared in similar advertisements. In an advertising campaign such as this, it is easy to see the connection between advertising, ideological ideas of female beauty, and filmmaking. Marketing products using the female body and marketing products to women to better beautify their own bodies both reinforce the idea that women's bodies are linked to products to be bought and sold. Cléo herself embodies both sides of this dichotomy: she luxuriates in the act of shopping for a hat, and, as a popular singer, she functions as an object used to sell commodities.

The film explores the pleasure that we associate with consumerism during the scene in which Cléo and Angèle shop for hats. The first shot of this scene occurs from inside the store looking out so that the many hats in the display window frame Cléo and Angèle. Varda then cuts to close-ups of both women as they look with pleasure and interest at different hats, which Varda then reveals in reverse shots. The montage of their looks and the hats in question, along with the emotional response from the women, suggests a familiar female ritual in which women bond over their love of shopping for feminine objects. In another shot, looking dreamily at herself in the mirror while trying on a hat, Cléo says to herself: "Everything suits me. Trying things on intoxicates me." As she says this, Varda shoots a close-up of her face as Cléo puts her hands on either side and looks dreamily at herself in this hat. In this way, she acts as the epitomé of ideal beauty so much so that not only do the products make her but she makes the products: everything looks stylish and beautiful on her. Shopping almost provides a high that erases momentarily the existential crisis that Cléo had been feeling moments beforehand.

The scene poses the question whether shopping actually gives Cléo agency and thus makes her into a subject rather than an object. How might consumerism be both oppressing women and liberating them at the same time? Is this possible? Varda's investigation into this foreshadows a trend in television and film in the 1990s and 2000s that suggests that women were in fact subjects with agency when they enjoyed their consumerism and when they earned their own money to consume these products. Varda shows this possibility but critiques it at the same time.

Contemporary versions of this idea, however, tend to glamorize this consumerism and reinforce that female empowerment meant the power to consume the products that would make you more feminine. The television series *Sex and the City* (1998–2004) represents the apex of this type of feminism. Some critics celebrate the series for investigating female sexual desire, but it always manages to fold this desire into an image of ideal femininity. In analyzing this series, feminist cultural theorist Angela McRobbie says, "the resolution of these possibly transgressive desires into a straightforward endorsement of the joys of consumption, made possible through the female wage, re-secures a scenario of gender normativity, merely adjusted to take into account the various advantages to the social order which come about through this independent economic activity."[19] Shows like *Sex and the City* as well as films, advertising, and magazines often present consumerism as both a freeing act and one that will lead the woman back to ideal femininity. This empowered approach to achieving ideal femininity continues to reinforce older patriarchal tropes in which society encourages women to spend their energy fitting within the limited role of ideal femininity rather than abandoning this role altogether.[20]

Varda does not celebrate this female consumerist pleasure nor does she simply denounce it through the film. Instead, she encourages the viewer to engage with the pleasure of consumption by creating a visually complex environment with mirrors that comment formally on Cléo's shopping. Varda also comments on it narratively by placing the shopping scene next to scenes about her death and by eventually leading Cléo away from the consumerist environment at the end of the film. Varda approaches what for feminism is a very political topic—ideal female beauty and its relationship to capitalism—through the form and plot structure rather than through overt dialogue. In this way, she asks the spectator to think through this rather than telling the spectator what to think. Nonetheless, Varda still presents an argument through the way that she poses the question: the contradictions of ideal beauty become apparent as the question of the pleasure that one takes in it arises.

In the shopping scene, Cléo strikes feminine poses for Angéle as she tries on the hats. Angéle adds another layer to the consumerist scene—that of the female viewer. Cléo's enjoyment is not just based on her enjoyment of her looks and the way the hats look on her but also on the fact that Angéle is watching her try them on. Often after putting a hat on she turns and displays it for Angéle, who nods approvingly. Angéle especially looks pleased with the way the shopping has cheered up Cléo. In this shot, Varda considers the way that ideal female beauty is as much cultivated by communities of women as by men.

The store has various square mirrors placed strategically for shoppers to admire themselves in. But they also provide added layers of signification. On the one hand, we see Cléo's reaction. On the other hand, the mirrors create an abstract landscape of female commodities, and Cléo is embedded into this landscape. Here, the distortion at the heart of beauty comes in the form of the fractured commodified female image that exists alongside the hats in the store. As Cléo wanders through the store, her image becomes increasingly fractured until a shot at the end reveals her image completely taken apart. In this shot, the reflection in a mirror shows a manikin's arm protruding through the middle of the square mirror with Cléo's face occupying the upper left corner and a small parasol she is carrying taking up the bottom left. Surrounding the square mirror are other aspects of the shop—a curtain, another mirror, a flower, as well as blurry items in the background—none of which come together in any meaningful way. The frame within a frame has no wholeness, and this indicates the fractured nature of Cléo's identity. Her face is just a small part of this collage of femininity that has no inherent coherence.

After this scene, Cléo and Angèle take a taxi and then go back to Cléo's apartment. There, they meet Cléo's boyfriend and the musicians. But after these interactions, Cléo takes off her wig, puts on a new hat, finds a simpler dress, and heads off by herself. This marks a significant change in Cléo's relationship to the ideal of female beauty, and this change becomes apparent through her interaction with a mirror.

Just into her walk, Cléo encounters herself in a mirror on the side of a Chinese restaurant. She says to herself: "My unchanging doll's face. This ridiculous hat." In this scene, the mirror plays the opposite role than the one that it played earlier in the film. The mirror here enables Cléo to begin to see her beauty as a negative rather than as the foundation of her vitality. Her unchanging beauty that so pleases her earlier and that her boyfriend assures her is the key to her health now is as ridiculous as the hat she purchased earlier. She has lost affection for both.

The Chinese lettering on the mirror acts as the obstacle that stands in the way of Cléo's direct access to herself. But this obstacle is not an external one; it is inherent to subjectivity itself. The subject can only see itself through the obstacle or distortion, and in this sense, the Chinese lettering reveals the true function of the mirror, despite their apparent contrast. Looking in the mirror, Cléo takes off her hat and says: "I can't see my own fears." This seems like a strange statement until she subsequently reveals her appearance as the source of her fears. She says: "I thought everyone looked at me. I only look at myself." These last lines express a crisis rooted directly in the ideology of beauty within patriarchy. She realizes here that the social order that she endlessly prepares herself for does not really exist. There is no one to look at her, and even when people do look at her, they see ideal beauty rather than Cléo. They see an ideological fantasy. This gives her status, but it also completely erases her at the same time.

The mirror in this scene reveals that Cléo has no one to see her and that she herself cannot be seen. Her looking in mirrors earlier in the film now becomes clear: she was always just looking at herself. The distortion of this mirror that emerges through the Chinese lettering allows Cléo to see what she couldn't see in the earlier mirrors—the truth of her subjectivity. For the spectator, the fracture of Cléo's subjectivity also becomes apparent. Rather than existing as a whole on the screen, Cléo appears divided in the image because Varda places the mirror behind the glass windows of the restaurant and surrounds it with white curtains that obscure the image of Cléo. Unlike earlier in the film, this scene enables the spectator's experience of Cléo's divided subjectivity to coincide with Cléo's own.

In this scene with the mirror at the Chinese restaurant, the film reveals again its attitude toward female beauty. Rather than embracing beauty or rejecting it, Varda argues for engaging this ideal in order to recognize what it can reveal. The point is to engage female beauty as an ideological fantasy in order to experience the inherent contradictions within it. Ideology offers every woman this split of being looked at and being erased by this very look. In each mirror scene, Cléo actively looks for herself, and this act of looking reveals her subjectivity—the fact that she is the only one who really sees what is happening to her, while everyone else just sees an ideal.

Dorothée and the final mirror

The next important mirror scene in *Cléo from 5 to 7* involves Cléo's friend Dorothée. Dorothée functions as a point of comparison with Cléo because she also makes money from her appearance by posing nude for art classes. And yet, there is a difference. Cléo comments multiple times that she couldn't do such a thing, that she would be too afraid that everyone would see her flaws, and that she finds posing nude too immodest. While on the one hand she embraces profiting from her own beauty on the other hand she can't embrace Dorothée's version of this. Dorothée, however, seems more carefree. She comments that she enjoys her body instead of being proud of it. This comment is a critique of Cléo since it is clear that she is quite proud of her looks and that they are the foundation for her symbolic identity.

In the way that she films Dorothée's nude body, Varda creates several layers of engagement for the spectator. Varda frames Dorothée's body in a way that emphasizes her nakedness as a mode of gesture, as an expression of subjectivity, rather than as a mode of turning the female body into an object. The effect of this is to mediate Dorothée as a sexual object to be looked at and thereby shift the traditional patriarchal way of looking at the female body. There are two ways Varda shapes the spectator's engagement with and frames Dorothée's body.

The first way begins before we see Dorothée. The camera leads the spectator through a room filled with sculptures that artists have created of people in various poses. The sculptures don't have small details and are instead created with broad strokes. Their emphasis is the gesture of the naked body. Here the camera is ostensibly from Cléo's point of view, and it moves in a slow traveling shot as Cléo walks through the room while encountering these large sculptures in different poses. One sculpture, for example, shows a woman swimming. On the sound track during this shot, one hears only Cléo's footsteps as she walks quietly through the room. This unbroken traveling shot forces the spectator to consider these unrealistic yet expressive sculptures of the human body as Cléo does. Through this shot, Varda already has the spectator engaging the body in a way that bypasses the traditional mode of objectification.

The second way Varda shapes the spectator's engagement with the female body in this scene occurs as Cléo enters the next room. The original traveling shot continues a bit further through the door into the room where the sculpture class is being held and where Dorothée is modeling. As Cléo steps through the door, the film cuts to a reverse shot of Cléo looking around for her friend. The shot again reverses, and Varda employs another traveling shot that is meant to approximate Cléo as she moves around the room to catch her friend's attention. This is again a quiet scene: the only sounds come from Cléo's shoes and the artists sculpting with chisels. This quietness of the scene allows the spectator to focus on the complexity of the visual field. The shot depicts a group of fifteen students with their teacher, as well as Dorothée modeling naked for them. As the shot moves, it reveals Dorothée suddenly when the camera passes one of the larger sculptures. She is standing on a block in the center of the room and is posing classically with one hand clasping the other behind her back, her hair up in a bun, and her left foot angled out just a little. It is a pose that clearly signals classical sculpture.

Varda frames Dorothée in a full shot so that the spectator sees her entire body from head to toe. In the shot, the spectator can plainly make out Dorothée's buttocks, the outline of her breast, and the profile of her face since she is turned just slightly. Additionally, the many sculptures that the students are making of Dorothée flank her in the shot. Some sculptures are close to the camera and obscure part of the view, while others are right next to Dorothée. But all of them reproduce Dorothée's body. This repeats the earlier scene in which the mirror provides an infinite repetition of Cléo's image. Here, the female body repeats multiple times, but the emphasis on the body is very different. In the mirror scene that repeats Cléo's body, the many iterations of Cléo's body suggest the signifying practice of beauty as well as the fracture within this practice. In this scene, Dorothée's beauty is a gesture of her body that is inspiring artistic expression. It is significant that the repetitions of Dorothée's beauty are not exact like mirror images. They do not treat her body as a consumer object but as a point of departure for artistic speculation. Framing Dorothée's nude body among the sculptures allows the spectator to engage in a comparison of her body and the artists renditions so that the spectator must spend more time evaluating the art than seeing Dorothée's body as the main spectacle.

In addition, the students, who are both men and women, look into the camera as Cléo passes them. They just briefly look at her as she passes, but they don't make note of her in the same way the men on the street do. When Cléo is finally standing in front of her friend, Dorothée turns and looks directly into the camera and tells Cléo that she will be finished momentarily. At this point, Varda includes the next chapter title—Chapter Nine: Dorothée from 5:52 to 6:00 p.m.—and reveals what Dorothée is thinking at that moment. This further frames Dorothée as a subject rather than an object by giving her direct address into the camera, naming her in the title, and allowing us to hear her thoughts (that she is happy Cléo has arrived). Dorothée gets dressed and prepares to leave. Though she exchanges goodbyes with the students and teacher, they do not focus on her body. We hear the teacher critiquing one of the students work, but it is the work he critiques, not Dorothée's body.

As Dorothée and Cléo walk out to her car, Cléo confesses that she could never do what Dorothée does. During this conversation, Varda further frames the previous nude shot of Dorothée by allowing Dorothée to explain her own feelings about being seen nude and being made into an art object. Dorothée says: "My body makes me happy, not proud. They're looking at more than just me ... a shape, an idea ..." Dorothée embraces the concept of her body as a shape and an idea but doesn't see that as defining her subjectivity.

Here, Varda frames the female body in multiple ways. She does this through introducing the sculptures first, employing a traveling shot that includes the sculptures and the students as well as Dorothée, and she wraps this visual investigation with a narrative element that allows Dorothée's character to explain how she sees herself. Varda's choices here emphasize engaging the female body through a mediation that is very different than the mainstream patriarchal objectification of the female body. This scene and the two after it function as turning points after which Cléo's journey and her engagement with her own identity begins to change.

Following this scene that introduces Dorothée, she drives along with Cléo to where Dorothée's boyfriend is projecting films. During the drive, Cléo confesses that she is sick and waiting for a diagnosis. Dorothée expresses concern but doesn't change her attitude toward Cléo. They arrive at the projection booth of the cinema and see Dorothée's boyfriend who also knows Cléo. He tells them that he is about to show a short and that they should watch it because it is amusing. The women look out the projection booth window, and Varda transitions to the film that is playing.

We see a silent short based on the style of Buster Keaton. Jean-Luc Godard, another member of the French New Wave, plays the main character. In the short film, the male character waves to his girlfriend who is running down the stairs. He then puts on sunglasses, and instead of just running down the stairs, she runs, trips, and dies. But at the end of the film, the male character takes off his sunglasses and realizes that he was seeing his life too bleakly. He sees the scene again, but this time his girlfriend just trips but doesn't die. The short film clearly pokes fun at Cléo's depression. The women turn away from the short film when it is over laughing and continue smiling as they leave the cinema. This is one of the few times we see Cléo smiling with pleasure. It seems the diversion of cinema has really lightened her mood, but this is short lived.

As Cléo and Dorothée leave the theater, Dorothée's purse spills and a mirror of hers falls to the ground and smashes. Cléo is horrified. She claims that the smashed mirror signifies death, and she finds herself immediately back in her existential dread. As Varda moves the camera in to the shattered mirror on the concrete, the spectator can see that Cléo's eye is reflected in one of the pieces. This is the final mirror scene, and it is the most fractured. Cléo's face is no longer just distorted but entirely obliterated, as only her eye remains staring back out of the fragments. This most fragmented mirror signifies a turning point, and the eye visible in the fragment of mirror is the key to the scenes that follow. In this light, Alison Smith argues that the first half of the film is about Cléo being looked at but the second half is about her looking. She says: "Cléo changes from object to be looked at to subject who looks and interprets what she looks at—from woman seen to woman seeing."[21] To add to Smith's point, we can note the way that the mirror is in many ways what signifies and even causes this turn.

Varda employs mirrors here because they are metaphorically at the center of the feminist question about ideal female beauty and its relationship to individual women. And rather than advocating eliminating mirrors altogether, Varda contends that our relationship to mirrors can change. She employs mirrors to add layers of visual information that prompts new interpretations from the spectator while at the same time symbolizing the fluctuations in Cléo's own relationship to femininity.

The mirrors also act as a way to frame the female body and redouble its presence in the visual field. What might start out as a traditional view of the woman's beauty—like in the hat shop—quickly turns into a distortion of the traditional view. Besides creating striking images, this has the effect of allowing the spectator to interpret the scene in a way that moves beyond just traditional expectations of enjoying her beauty. The scene prompts the viewer both to explore the new meaning that comes out of unusual juxtapositions of objects as well as to critique Cléo's relationship to her own beauty. She clearly seems somewhat narcissistic, but Varda doesn't allow the spectator to entirely dismiss Cléo, even when her narcissism is evident. This is important because it allows Varda to engage the spectator beyond identification and to prompt the spectator to see her own investment in the idea of ideal beauty.

Le Dôme Café and its indifference

Though mirrors are not a central focus of the scene that takes place in Le Dôme Café in Montparnasse, Paris, this scene fits alongside the mirror scenes because of its focus on looking or being looked at. In fact, it is a very strange moment for Cléo and one that unsettles her as much as her encounters with mirrors. She heads to Le Dôme after she leaves her own apartment (where she visits with her boyfriend and rehearses her songs). She enters the café wearing her sunglasses as if she is afraid to be recognized and just wants to be left alone. This is a legitimate fear since wherever she goes, people either stare at her for her beauty or fuss over her because she is a popular singer. Her fame and popularity seem to be as much tied to her voice as they are tied to her good looks, which fit into the patriarchal ideology's ideal of female beauty.

The scene in Le Dôme is strange, however, for the singular reason that no one looks at her. This is not something that the spectator notices right away. If anything, Cléo might notice this before the spectator. But as she walks around and around the café supposedly looking for a place to sit, finding someplace, changing her mind, walking more and finding another place, the spectator becomes increasingly aware of the people at the café not noticing Cléo. It is almost as if she purposely keeps walking closely by the tables to see if anyone will either recognize her or at the very least look at her for her beauty, but no one does either.

Varda shoots this scene with a lot of movement as she follows Cléo. The shots flow back and forth in moving shot/reverse shot sequences to record the people Cléo is passing and her response to them. As Cléo passes each table, the spectator hears snippets of the people's conversation. This visual aesthetic is different than in earlier scenes, and it is a difference that engages the spectator to consider why things have changed. As Steven Ungar says, "whereas the visual perspective in the earlier film was often fixed in one spot, the fluid camera movement in this chapter simulates Cléo's gaze as she walks in the café and down the streets that surround it."[22] In this way, the spectator has many clues to believe that she is seeing what Cléo is seeing.

While normally theorists would talk about identification here, the scene that unfolds provides enough layers that identification with Cléo becomes more of a multilayered engagement involving the interpretation of the visuals, dialogue, and response of Cléo to the people in the café. Either Cléo seems to be registering what the people in the café are saying or Varda is actually directing the snippets of conversation at the spectator. The conversations in Le Dôme are either about art, politics, or relationships, and they seem to represent an array of topics important to France at that moment, including modernist painting and the Algerian War. Hearing these conversations has the effect of diminishing Cléo's own concerns. Her worries do not take center stage amid the myriad problems that the patrons of the café discuss.

Cléo goes to the jukebox and plays one of her songs in an effort to garner attention. But no one seems to notice except one young woman who says that the loud music prevents her from paying attention to the conversation. Thus, the only attention Cléo can elicit from the crowd at the café is negative, though the predominant response is indifference. In the middle of the sequence, she sits at a table that is near a pole covered with little mirrors. Her face is reflected in all these fragments, but this time she does not notice. In the first café scene, she attracts a lot of attention, and the waiters pamper her. And yet, she turns around and tries to find herself in the mirror there. But in this scene where no one notices her, she does not worry about finding herself in the mirror or worry about the mirror reflecting her image back in a fractured manner. The juxtaposition between these two scenes and how the attention Cléo receives affects her own anxiety about her image provokes a philosophical and feminist question.

Not receiving attention makes Cléo restless. She clearly notices the lack of attention, but it also does not provoke the kind of crisis that she experienced earlier. Film theorists Alison Smith and Steven Ungar—in their two different books on Varda and *Cléo from 5 to 7*, respectively—both see this scene as one that emphasizes Cléo's looking rather than being looked at and that this is the significant difference in this scene. Smith argues: "The people that she encounters allow her to forget herself in other subjectivities, to look at alternative lives."[23] Smith then suggests that this continues even more as she meets with her friend Dorothée and encounters Antoine at the end of the film. It is certainly correct that in this scene at Le Dôme, Varda embeds a different emphasis, one of Cléo looking and not being seen, into a visually rich environment with compelling dialogue that enables the spectator to engage with the film on multiple levels. But it is not clear that Cléo has overcome the fact of being looked at or that overcoming being looked at functions as a feminist ideal.

While watching this scene, the spectator can consider how Cléo's identity is shaped by her interactions with the people and environment around her, as well as focus on Cléo's own thoughts and desires. The film here foregrounds the question: how is our identity formed between the balance of our relationship with other people and our internal experience, thoughts, and desires? What does it take to shift or change the way we think of ourselves or the way others think of us, and how much is looking and being looked at a part of this? Is being looked at an inextricable part of looking? As much as Cléo is worried about cancer, this prognosis of potential death sends her into an investigation that has as much to do with her relationship to ideal beauty and her relationship with other people, as it does with the cancer itself.

On location shooting and the streets of Paris

Another space in which looking and being looked at occurs regularly are on the streets of Paris. In fact, the streets of Paris play a key role throughout the entire film. There are scenes interspersed throughout the film depicting Cléo on her own or with her friends walking or driving in Paris. These scenes provide Cléo passage from one space to another, for example, the streets are featured when Cléo goes from the first café to the hat store and from one interior space to another, but they themselves also are important scenes in their own right. The street scenes provide a site where Varda can demonstrate how looking and being looked at take place.

The streets for Cléo are a place for contemplation and observation, a place where she can think about herself while looking at others. She tends to look to the hustle and bustle on the streets to calm herself and occupy her mind in order to quiet her existential angst. While on the street, she is not shopping but instead watching people and being looked at. The people on the street not only look at Cléo but also look directly into the camera lens. This indicates that those who react to Cléo on the street are not actors in Varda's film. They are just people who happen to pass by at the moment when Varda films the various scenes, and this fact gives the film a documentary flavor.

Varda's use of location shooting with actual crowds places *Cléo from 5 to 7* firmly in the aesthetic of the French New Wave movement. One of the main tenets of this movement was that location shooting allowed for a more realistic look that countered the glamorous lighting of the studio popular in commercial French cinema. Unlike Italian Neorealism, which privileged realism above all else, the French New Wave saw realism as part of its overall aesthetic. Realism was not a goal in itself.

New Wave directors juxtaposed the realism of location shooting with formal innovations that had the effect of disrupting realism rather than augmenting it. This juxtaposition creates a unique style that provokes spectator reflection on the reality depicted in the films. For her part, Varda employs a version of these aesthetics when she uses jump cuts when Cléo is driving or formally distorts the mirrors in the image. She also positions radically different scenes next to each other in the film's chronology.

The stylized scenes from Cléo's apartment sit side by side with the realist street scenes. The experience of moving between these two very different styles can be jarring or at the very least demands interpretation from the spectator. Through this juxtaposition, Varda engages spectators by asking them to create the link between these different styles of filmmaking. In the one scene, it seems as if we could be watching a melodramatic romance or women's film, and then in the very next scene it's as if we are in an Italian Neorealist film or a documentary. Popular cinema generally tries for consistency of style in order to hide the seams of the film and keep the spectator ensconced in the film's plot. In other words, this cinema creates form that is subservient to content. But the French New Wave in general and Varda specifically develop a form that acts as a commentary on the content. The spectator learns as much from the form as from the movement of the plot. In Varda's *Cléo from 5 to 7*, the formal juxtapositions continually highlight the tension within ideal beauty between looking and being looked at. Varda shows that this ideological fantasy of female beauty develops on the basis of Cléo's idea of herself as much as by the way the social order treats her.

Varda's choice to leave the people looking at her camera in the film is particularly revealing. People stare at Cléo, and they stare at the camera. Sometimes they first look at Cléo and then look at the camera, and sometimes they seem to look at Cléo because they notice the camera following her. This leads them to scrutinize the camera itself and the camera operator, whom the spectator can't see. Popular cinema avoids showing this type of activity because the fear is that these looks will pull the spectator out of the story itself and make her aware of the camera and the production process as a whole. But this is not what happens in Varda's film, and she does not aim at producing alienation in the spectator by including these looks at the camera. Varda concerns herself instead with how the looks might further engage the spectator rather than distance the spectator. As spectators, we are also in the system of looking and being looked at that envelops Cléo. We participate in looking, as we would in any film, but we also find ourselves as part of the visual field. The spectator experiences the look and the being looked at.

In this way, Varda creates a tension in which the spectator is identifying with both the subject and object position. Being caught in between these two positions allows her to see the antagonism of subjectivity itself. Looking and being looked at are how we figure out the difference between subject and other. In other words, looking signifies the subject and the experience of being looked at signifies the existence of the other. But looking and being looked at can never overlap. We both look and are looked at, but we can never occupy both positions at the same time.

Varda highlights the interaction of looking and being looked at by making her film about the complex system of looks. People have a more direct relationship to looking, even though looking is not a pure act but one mediated by the psyche. We seem to know intuitively what constitutes looking. And at the same time, we have no idea how we are being looked at, except in our fantasy about how others see us. But without the sense of being looked at, we would not be able to look. Our looking depends on the fact that we are seen, and our being seen depends on our looking, even though the two acts can never coincide. This is the foundational antagonism that defines subjectivity, and it is also at the center of Varda's film.

Being looked at can be traumatic—it can also be pleasurable—because we cannot know how the other is looking at us. The other's look at us is a blank spot in our psychic world, but our subjectivity depends on it. For women this is especially fraught because patriarchy as an ideology puts women in the position of being looked at. As much as feminists from different moments in history have wanted to, we cannot destroy this aspect of femaleness because it is an essential aspect of subjectivity as such. Nor can we simply take it up as a banner under which to march and claim that we revel in our objectification, that we actually enjoy it. We can, however, shift the contours of how we define "to be looked at." Varda participates in this process by including the looks of the people on the street. As the film progresses, she also includes more of Cléo's point of view of the people on the street, which becomes another marker of Cléo's own sense of awareness.

Varda employs a complex system of mainstream and experimental looks to emphasize the nature of the patriarchal system women are caught in as well as to gesture toward ways to question it. She engages the spectator to see the intersections so that the tenets of ideal beauty can begin to fall apart. The ideal of female beauty relies heavily on the idea that this beauty will transform her into a precious object that everyone will cherish. This leaves little room for women to look themselves. Popular cinema has a real paucity of examples of women looking in connection with being looked at. By depicting Cléo both looking and being looked at, as well as including the startling looks at the camera itself, Varda engages the spectator and prompts her to consider their role in this process.

On the streets of Paris, Cléo has several encounters that highlight the intersection between looking and being looked at. Most often, these encounters shock Cléo, and they emphasize the trauma of being looked at. But Cléo clearly wants the other's attention. Her popularity and financial success depends on other people adoring her. On the other hand, Cléo's encounters with strangers—the very strangers she relies on to like her songs—are not pleasant, and even the non-traumatic encounters leave her indifferent.

Two of the encounters are with street performers. Different times while walking, Cléo sees people crowded around a performer. The first performer is eating live frogs. When she recognizes what he is doing, Cléo stares fascinated and disgusted. Varda provides several close-ups of his face with the frog legs sticking out. Cléo walks away upset and then walks into Le Dôme, where no one looks at her. Afterward, she walks away from the café and heads to see her friend Dorothée. On the way, she runs into many crowded spaces and then notices another street performer. Rather than eating live frogs, this one is sticking a huge nail through his bicep. Cléo stays for less time to see this; she experiences the event itself as an attack and runs away from the crowd with a horrified look on her face. The enjoyment that the crowd finds in these horrific events, an enjoyment that makes no sense to Cléo, traumatizes her. The fact that the spectators find enjoyment in bodily mutilation proves especially troublesome for her. They activate her own fears about her body betraying her by becoming cancerous.

Another important encounter happens more toward the beginning of the film with a taxi driver. Angèle and Cléo take a taxi after the hat shop and discover their taxi driver is a woman. Having a woman working in a predominantly male job represents a significant choice on Varda's part since it emphasizes female independence. While in the taxi, Varda includes shots of Paris (again all documentary in style since the crowds are the real crowds of Paris not actors), while we hear the conversation with the taxi driver and the news on the radio. One of the first things to occur during their taxi ride is that two men in a car start to pass them, notice Cléo, and then whistle at her. One of the men even tries to reach out and touch her. This sequence highlights Cléo's objectification because it occurs while she is in the seeming privacy of a taxi. She is used to this kind of attention, however, and laughs it off. Nonetheless, the moment further drives home the way that the social order constantly reinforces her identity.

The taxi driver turns on the radio and one of Cléo's songs envelops them in the car. Cléo complains bitterly about the quality of the recording and asks the taxi driver to turn it off. This moment further enhances not only the idea that Cléo really is quite famous but also that the public is a place where she constantly encounters representations of who she supposedly is—a beautiful talented singer. The men whistling in the car and the song on the radio reveal that she is seen in a particular way by the social order.

Cléo also works to perpetuate how she is seen, but the security of how the social order sees her breaks down throughout the film. The possible diagnosis of cancer, which Cléo is sure she will hear at the end of the day, has thrown this all askew. Now she looks at herself in the mirror and sees distortions rather than perfections. She begins to wonder who she is and why she is not seen as she wants to be seen. Feeling distanced from her own song on the radio continues this sense of alienation from her public image.

The discussion with the taxi driver highlights Cléo's increasing distance from her own position as a woman being looked at. Angèle comments that being a taxi driver is dangerous for a woman and the woman agrees that it is sometimes dangerous but that she likes it nonetheless. Cléo says, "Aren't you afraid at night?" The taxi driver asks what she would be afraid of, but then goes on to tell a story about being attacked the past winter. She explains that two students wouldn't pay so she ran after them, but they turned to attack her. She locked herself in her car and radioed for help. Two colleagues answered the call and scared them away. Cléo responds with, "Weren't you scared to death?" and the taxi driver replies, "I'm not the fearful type." This exchange is the most overtly feminist moment in the film. The female taxi driver is taking a job in a mostly male profession. It is also a profession in which you are alone with all kinds of people and potentially vulnerable to them.

This exchange emphasizes that one aspect of being a woman, which Cléo is clearly attuned to, is vulnerability and potential physical harm. But it also suggests that the taxi driver doesn't have any fear and can confront potential threats when they arrive. Cléo and the taxi driver appear as polar opposites in the way that they take up femininity. The film doesn't condemn either approach, but it clearly presents the female taxi driver as a kind of hero on the streets of Paris. The taxi driver mentions that the entire incident made the newspapers and thus indicates her response to feminine vulnerability, though a minority position, has made its way into the public realm.

The taxi driver represents a clear challenge to Cléo's attempt to embody the ideal of female beauty and to accept the vulnerability that accompanies it. Varda includes this scene in the film to show the spectator that Cléo's approach is not the only possibility and that the alternatives are easily thinkable. After Angèle and Cléo leave the taxi, Angèle comments that the taxi driver was quite a character, and Cléo expresses her shock at what the taxi driver said. Angèle counters by noting that the taxi driver had courage. But Cléo cannot avow this because the taxi driver challenges her being in the world through her different approach to femininity.

Just after the taxi driver recounts the story of the robbery in the taxi, she turns on the radio. The rest of the ride consists of the shots of Cléo and Angèle in the cab, the street scenes they are looking at, and the sound of the news program and commercials. Varda includes this lengthy ride with no dialogue and no plot development in order to provide a contemplative moment in which the spectator can mull over the taxi driver's story along with Cléo's response to it. During this moment that Varda sets aside for reflection, the first item that we hear on the radio is an advertisement for shampoo. The advertisement announces a new shampoo for American women made of whisky. It says, "Whisky revitalizes the hair." As it says this, Varda cuts to a shot of Angèle patting her hair. This nod to the way that advertising reinforces conceptions of ideal female beauty comes directly in the wake of the story of the very courageous female taxi driver in order to suggest the myriad of opposing responses to the feminine ideal. Varda uses this juxtaposition to encourage the spectator to see the incongruities, to see the gaps between the way we see and the way we are looked at, or to see the distinction between ideological messages and lived experience.

The signs of Algeria

The conflict between opposed responses to the ideal of femininity takes place in *Cléo from 5 to 7* against the background of a geopolitical conflict occurring at the time.

This latter conflict makes its presence felt in the film during the taxi ride. After we hear the shampoo advertisement, the rest of the radio program playing during the taxi ride focuses on the French war in Algeria. The Algerian War was a war between Algeria and France from 1954 to 1962, which led ultimately to Algeria gaining its independence from France. The anti-colonial uprising and the brutal French response involved terrorism, guerilla warfare, and barbaric torture. The end of the war marked the end of France's colonial rule over Algeria that began in the 1830s.

The brutality of the French colonial forces turned the Algerians completely against them and even led a large part of the French population to oppose the war. Intellectuals spoke out against French activities in Algeria, and artists used their works to demonstrate their outrage. Several French filmmakers critically addressed the Algerian War, including Jean-Luc Godard in *Le Petit Soldat* (*The Little Soldier*, 1960). Because Godard's film depicts French cruelty and shows torture occurring on both sides, authorities banned the film from public screening until 1963. Alain Renais made *Muriel ou le Temps d'un retour* (*Muriel, or the Time of a Return*) which was also released in 1963, a film that, like *Cléo from 5 to 7*, contains oblique references to the war. The film depicts a man haunted by participating in the torture of a woman named Muriel during the war. Renais had also been one of the signatories of the *Manifesto of 121*, a group opposed to the military's actions in Algeria. The members of the group included Simone de Beauvoir, André Breton, Guy Debord, Marguerite Duras, Claude Lanzmann, Jean-Paul Sartre, and François Truffaut. The group published their manifesto and names as a protest on September 6, 1960 in the magazine *Vérité-Liberté*.

In the future, Varda would make overtly political documentaries, such as her film on the Black Panthers and her short included in *Loin du Vietnam* (*Far from Vietnam*, 1967), in which seven filmmakers made films against the American war in Vietnam. She remained convinced, however, that this was not the way to get a large portion of the public to think about the issues. In an interview with Varda in 1977, journalist Gerald Peary asked her about her approach to her film *L'une chante, l'autre pas* (*One Sings, the Other Doesn't*, 1977). She explains, "Make it clear, simple, not too complicated. If I put myself on the screen—very natural and feminist—maybe I'd get ten people in the audience. Instead, I put two nice young females on the screen, and not too much of my own leftist conscience. By not being too radical but truly feminist, my film has been seen by 350,000 people in France. It's better if they all got half the message than to have 5,000 people seeing a courageous 16 mm film."[24] This makes it quite clear that Varda's project is trying to reach the largest possible audience. Thus, her use of the form to articulate a point was both a measure of her artistic vision and a way to approach politically charged issues without alienating her potential audience. And this is exactly how she approaches the Algerian War, which has a presence that is woven throughout the story of Cléo, in *Cléo from 5 to 7*.

The topic of the Algerian War does not have a primary position in the narrative of the film but appears in snippets in unexpected places. The radio sequence in the taxi is one of these places. The news report in fact goes through several aspects of unrest in France at the time: the Algerian War, a strike and protest by farmers, and 4,000 protesters shouting "Liberate Breton" (advocating for Brittany to be its own country). The news report about the Algerian War mentions that there was more rioting in Algeria and gives the casualties for that day (twenty dead and sixty wounded). Then the report mentions a military tribunal. The presentation of this report suggests that the French experienced details about the war on a daily basis and that this horrific information became a routine part of daily French life.

The question for Varda is what relationship do we take up to this kind of information. The Algerian War took place far from Paris, but nonetheless its implications bore on everyone in France and interrupted Parisian life. Cléo seems utterly unaffected by the news report, but later when she meets and bonds with Antoine, a soldier about to return to Algeria, she becomes more emotional and begins to have an opinion about the war. During the taxi ride, however, she and her ideal beauty seem undisturbed, as she listens to the collage of the radio program that puts Cléo's own song side by side with a shampoo commercial and a news report of the deaths taking place in Algeria on that day.

There is another aspect of this scene that comments on France's relationship to Algeria and to Africa in general. Earlier in the taxi ride, Cléo looks two different times out the window and sees stores specializing in African art and artifacts. In the window of the first store, the film shows traditional African masks, and rather than showing the masks from the distance that Cléo sees them, Varda shoots them in a close-up. This is slightly different than the treatment of the rest of the street scenes, which Varda shoots from the passenger's point of view. The next instance is similar and occurs a little later in the ride. Cléo looks out the window and again sees a store with African artifacts. The camera initially shoots this from inside the cab, and Varda then shows Cléo look out the window. Cléo subsequently turns and looks forward, so that she is not looking at the store any longer. Varda emphasizes that Cléo looks away before she cuts to a close-up of the masks in the second storefront window. This unmistakably indicates that Varda positions the two close-up shots of the masks that follow for the spectator's look rather than Cléo's.

There are multiple racially charged implications at work during this sequence. Though these news reports and visual sightings seem to be in the background, the film has already established that what happens around Cléo bears on her own struggles. The external world in the film is separate from Cléo, but it constantly impacts her and reveals what she hides from herself. In this case, Varda links racial prejudices to Cléo's struggle with the ideal of female beauty. France's ideological commitment to its superiority to African colonies has its complement in the ideal of white female beauty, which feeds the fantasy of this superiority as well as the fantasy of a vulnerability that then requires violent defense. Varda sets these ideologies side by side to prompt the spectator to see the connections, and she uses this formal juxtaposition rather than explicit denunciation in order to engage rather than alienate the spectator.

The masks play a crucial role in the film's critique of the Algerian War. They show that while France is involved in the brutal colonization of African countries, it at the same time fetishizes African artifacts. The fetishization serves as the ideological background for colonization and enables it to continue. This observation about colonial ideology appears in a later film from Senegalese director Ousmane Sembène. In *Black Girl* (1966), often considered the first African feature film, Sembène shows how the love for African artifacts is used in the service of the oppression of actual Africans. The film is about a young Senegalese woman, Diouana (Mbissine Thérèse Diop), who moves to France to work for a French family as a nanny. She looks forward to the excitement of France but instead is treated harshly by the couple. They force her to work as a maid rather than as a nanny and thus completely alienate her. Throughout the film the image of an African mask that Diouana gives the family when she first arrives, recurs. The couple hangs the mask on their wall along with other pieces of African art. During a dinner party in which the couple has her serve them, Diouana realizes that she herself functions as another artifact for the family to display in order to impress their friends. In the end, she takes the mask back and kills herself. This tale of the devastating effects of colonialism appeared four years after the end of the Algerian War. Even though the films depict different countries and circumstances, the commonality remains for the effects of colonization. Varda's inclusion of the African masks and the news about Algeria also suggests that for the French people the countries in

Africa blur together as part of a general refusal to see past their own racist assumptions.

Varda also includes a similar reference in a scene in Le Dôme, which Cléo enters after this taxi ride, where two men discuss the Algerian War. The café is known as a hangout of artists and intellectuals, and the scene in the café is the most diverse scene in the film. It depicts people of different racial and ethnic backgrounds, bohemian fashions, and at least three different languages spoken. But even here, the discussion of the Algerian War is oddly ambivalent though revelatory. It occurs when Cléo is choosing a song on the jukebox. Varda keeps her in the shot the entire time in the background of a medium long shot that encompasses two men at a table and Cléo in the background at the jukebox. This is an important inclusion because it further suggests that Varda wants to link Cléo to the issue of the Algerian War. One bohemian older man says to his friend, "This Algerian craziness ... you don't know where you stand." The man seems genuinely depressed and anxious, as if the Algerian War has moved him into a state of existential crisis. Cléo looks at them, puts her sunglasses on, and moves on. She attempts to leave the issue behind her, but it recurs just like the cancer diagnosis.

In fact, the film links the cancer diagnosis with the war. Both represent potential imminent death, and both interrupt the fabric of everyday life. Cléo desperately tries to return to her former everydayness, but the anxiety that cancer brings with it prevents this. It has begun to unravel her carefully crafted ideal femininity and provoked her into a state of questioning antithetical to her former sense of her self. In the same way, French society cannot escape the background of the Algerian War and the death transpiring there. The Algerian War reveals to France the cost of the culture that it so prizes. Much of French belief in its own superiority had its basis in the colonial relationships it had with African countries. But the Algerian War, the torture, and massacres brought the violence of these relationships to the public fore and could no longer be ignored. Varda does not show protestors or radical action; instead, she tries to link the existential angst of France itself to that of Cléo, revealing the tenuousness of both.

Feminism, as Varda practices it in *Cléo from 5 to 7*, involves seeing how the contradictions that inform femininity manifest themselves in other aspects of the social order. One cannot insist solely on the feminist struggle while turning a blind eye to the violence of the Algerian War or the ramifications of French racism. As Varda conceives it in her film, there is a direct link between the ideal of female beauty and the vicious racism that the French practice toward Africa. But the struggle against this oppressive conjunction cannot be a straightforward one. The filmmaker interrupts the conjunction of sexism and racism rather than confronting it directly, and this interruption implies a distortion of chronological temporality.

Narrative structure and time

Prior to *Cléo from 5 to 7*, Alain Resnais had begun to experiment with alternative temporality in his films, most famously in *L'année dernière à Marienbad* (*Last Year at Marienbad*, 1961). Resnais's film shows the past constantly intruding on the present, so that eventually the spectator cannot tell when the events on the screen are taking place. Varda's film does not interrupt temporality in quite so dramatic a fashion, but she nevertheless indicates that a chronological conception of temporality misleads us into thinking that events have an unbroken narrative thread that they do not have.

The basic structure of *Cléo from 5 to 7* is rigidly chronological. It is a chronological presentation of two hours in one woman's life. The guideposts for the narrative are the chapter titles presented as subtitles throughout the film. The chapter titles—for example, "Cléo from 5:05 to 5:08" ("Cléo de 17 h. 05 A 17 h. 08")—are often a character's name and the amount of time the scene will last. In this way, Varda calls attention to the idea that the film is shot in real time or that the narrative will be responsible for real time. The spectator is thus aware of the relationship of Cléo's inner struggles and to the passage of time. Cléo does not necessarily have an aim. She does not have an appointment at the end of the two hours, though she is supposed to check in with her doctor around the end of the day.

While the titles keep us aware of the time, there is not a literal ticking clock that would make us feel a sense of urgency to time. No one in the film checks the time very often or comments that they must hurry or says that time is running out, as is common in films that emphasize the time as essential to the plot. Real time urgency has become a more common staple in very contemporary television shows and films such 24 (2001–2010) and John Badham's *Nick of Time* (1995). In the 1960s, this was relatively rare as a narrative device. One famous example in early cinema is Alfred Hitchcock's *Rope* (1948). But the central concern in *Rope* is the minimization of the cuts—creating the illusion that the film occurs without a cut—rather than creating a film in real time. Real time was a side effect of shooting without any obvious cuts. The result is a film that uses time to dramatic effect: even though there is no clock ticking as in *24*, time runs out for the main figures in *Rope* just as it does for the federal agents in the television series.

In *Cléo from 5 to 7*, however, real time does not serve to create tension. Instead, the film revolves around the interactions between Cléo and her friends. Though the time of Cléo's life may be running out due to the cancer in her body, the clock in the film does not remind the spectator of her impending death. Instead, it seems to regulate the events of Cléo's day, to provide a rigid separation between the different events that she experiences. The clock is not ticking in the film, despite the constant indicators of time passing.[25]

As I mentioned earlier, the phrase "cinq à sept" ("5 to 7") in France has a colloquial meaning of a reference to an afternoon love affair. In this case, Cléo is having an afternoon affair with the possibility of death. Varda leaves the spectator to question whether the title is trivializing this turn that Cléo takes with existential crisis or whether this is the affair that changes everything for Cléo and breaks her out of her ideological unawareness. Rather than present the narrative of this real time story as abiding by a ticking clock, Varda presents the story as small packages of time that make up Cléo's late afternoon, and each chapter has the potential to disrupt that time, even if they do also follow the clock. The clock itself serves to remind the spectator of time itself, and an individual's relationship to time as existential as well as practical. At the conclusion of the film, there is a disruption, and it seems that the accumulation of experiences, rather than one specific experience, causes it. The temporal disruption occurs when the film ends. The title promises a film transpiring between the hours of 5:00 p.m. and 7:00 p.m., but Varda does not finish the two hours. She actually ends the film after ninety minutes. This abrupt ending that breaks the promise of the title works to emphasize the ruptures that have happened in her life during these past wanderings.

The early ending is another disruption that connects to and highlights the rest of the disruptions in the film. It also shows Varda's adherence to the aesthetic of the French New Wave, which celebrated thwarting traditional expectations of film endings and resolutions. The title sets up our expectations of following *Cléo from 5 to 7*, and by thwarting this expectation Varda prompts the spectator to engage with the experience and consider why it ended early. The early ending deprives the spectator of a clear resolution, just as it deprives Cléo of a clear diagnosis and prognosis for her disease. By ending the film early, Varda indicates that while alive the narrative that we experience is always on the verge of being interrupted, and we must be ready for interruption.

In part, the experience of time in this film has to do with the varied types of editing and filmic styles that Varda employs. She does not rely solely on continuity editing or long takes. Instead, she provides a variety of editing styles dependent on the mood and characters of each scene. The beginning of the film signals this approach and sets the stage for the way the spectator begins to think of her engagement with the film. The most notable aspect of the beginning of the film is that it is in color while the rest of the film is not. One rarely sees the juxtaposition of color photography with black and white, and when it appears, it always has a clear thematic significance—such as distinguishing between the fantasy world and reality in *The Wizard of Oz* (Victor Fleming, 1939).

In the opening sequence, the tarot cards appear in color. Varda also shows us the reader's hands and Cléo's hands in color, but when the film cuts to their faces, it also cuts to black and white. This marks the only moment of color photography in the entire film. Varda employs color to represent the prediction and possibility rather than reality. As the film unfolds, we realize that this possibility of death pervades every gesture and experience for Cléo so that the tarot card reading becomes Cléo's lived fear. The color scene at the beginning of the film suggests a rupture of Cléo's identity, which the rest of the film depicts her attempting to integrate.

The turn from color to black and white at the beginning of the film has garnered considerable critical attention. Commenting on this switch, Steven Ungar suggests, "The contrast is coded as a mark of difference between the symbolic order of the tarot and the physical world of daily life in which Cléo has come to consult the fortune teller Irma."[26] One way to see how these worlds affect each other is in the way that the tarot reading, its suggestion of death, invades the rest of the film. The shift to black and white combined with the few shots that follow to make up this first sequence signal the nontraditional nature of this film's form and presentation of linear time. The film may stay carefully within the real time precept, but its shot structure is an untraditional way of representing time. This creates an inherent contradiction in the film, one which Varda is carefully crafting. In Varda's later film *The Beaches of Agnès*, she comments on this very tension in *Cléo from 5 to 7* when she says, "I wanted the film to combine objective time, as seen on the omnipresent clocks, and subjective time as Cléo experiences it during the film." Thus, Varda concentrates on this contradiction between private experience and public time as a way to express her character's questioning journey in the form itself. It is a contradiction that emphasizes the contradictions between the individual and the expectations of the social order. And in the case of Cléo, this very much revolves around the social order's expectations of female beauty and her own lived experience of her contradicting desires and anxieties that come into contact with these expectations of the larger society that she encounters as she travels through the city.

After the film changes from color to black and white, Cléo leaves the tarot reader's apartment. As she walks down the building's stairs, Varda shoots this with three repetitions of the same shot in the middle of her movement down the stairs. The insertion of this repetition immediately signals a creative use of reality and prompts the spectator to engage with what this might mean about Cléo's state of mind rather than just a document of her passage out of the building.[27] The repetition of the scene shows time as interruptive rather than chronological. The beginning of the film combines the switch of color to black and white with the single shot repeated three times, and the scene ends with Cléo looking into a mirror that reduplicates her image many times. These elements all prompt the spectator to contemplate what the form is suggesting about Cléo herself. Is she lost? How is she affected by the tarot reading? What do her beauty and her idea of herself have to do with her ability to take in this news? And why does the news lead to her need to assert her beauty? Varda suggests these questions by employing unusual choices even though under the aegis of documenting the minute-to-minute movement of Cléo from 5:00 p.m. to 7:00 p.m.

Cléo and Antoine

The conclusion of the film thwarts the spectator's expectations because Cléo seeks solace by isolating herself in a park and ends up finding it in the company of a stranger named Antoine.

In this final segment of the film, many of the themes from throughout return but in a seemingly different environment, which suggests that Cléo herself is beginning to see things differently. She goes to the park to be alone, and she chooses the paths that are mostly empty to walk on. At this point, the film's mise-en-scène and pacing present a new calm that Cléo seems to feel. When she stops at a stream to contemplate her problems, Antoine walks up to her. He leans in close to her and begins to make small talk. She tries to be polite but also to deflect the conversation. At one point, Antoine points out that it is the longest day of the summer and that the sun is moving from Gemini to Cancer. Just hearing the word cancer upsets Cléo and she sharply asks him to stop talking.

This response alerts Antoine that something is wrong, and he gently asks her several questions in order to understand. Answering one of his inquiries, she says that she's not waiting for anyone, and he replies that he isn't waiting for anyone either. She replies, "But all men wait for women. Then they speak to them. I don't usually reply. Today I forgot. My thoughts are elsewhere." This exchange suggests that for a moment she was not thinking of herself as a woman who is a beautiful object that men would want to possess. Normally, she suggests here, she is very aware of this and does not respond to this male attention unless she wants to, but in this case she was thinking about death so Antoine caught her off guard.

It is a moment that reinforces the question of one's relationship to female beauty that runs throughout the film. Varda seems to suggest that death naturally disrupts the ideology of beauty and throws it into relief. This prompts the person to recognize the structures that they had before been living in unquestioningly. In other words, the encounter with death prompts a questioning stance toward ideology. For Cléo, it allows her to forget her object status and expose herself to the other. Though this leads to her being open to her encounter with Antoine, the encounter with Antoine ends up leading back to ideology since his attention to her remains somewhat traditional: he appreciates her beauty and wants to protect her. Once Antoine understands that she is afraid of a diagnosis of cancer, he offers to go to the hospital with her if she will come and see him off at the train station where he will return to his tour of duty with the French Army in the Algerian War. Cléo agrees to this arrangement.

The scenes with Antoine are split into three separate scenes or spaces: the park, the bus, and the hospital grounds. In the park, Antoine convinces Cléo to his deal of accompanying each other on their rather sad errands. On the bus, Antoine asks Cléo for her photo so that he can look at it while he is at war, and she gives it to him. On the hospital grounds, Cléo asks Antoine for his address so that she can write to him and he gives it to her. These exchanges, along with the many looks, physical touching, and jokes that they share, suggest that Cléo is attracted to Antoine. She begins to fall for him and to rely on him emotionally.

But this sequence of events contradicts what the film has been leading up to. That is to say, the previous segments of the film all detail bouts with existential angst, the disruption of Cléo's mirror image, and traumatic encounters with strangers and friends. These events lead her to question whether people really see her or care about her at all, but at the end of the film, she envisions herself being saved by a man who reminds her how pleasurable it is to be adored as a beautiful woman and taken care of. Considering all that has come before, Varda seems to have veered far from feminism with this ending.

As feminists have pointed out, narratives about women often have few options for endings. One of the primary resolutions that popular narratives offer is that women find romance, and this solves many if not all of their problems. In this sense, the end of *Cléo from 5 to 7* seems to fit perfectly within patriarchy's assumptions about women. After an hour and half of self-investigation and some steps forward in which Cléo begins to take up the position of looking rather than only being looked at, it seems odd to finish the film with Cléo finding a man who makes her feel better by asking for her photo and devoting himself to her. This does not, however, encompass the entirety of the ending since the spectator is also aware of other aspects that contradict this neatly contrived romantic ending.

At the very end, in fact, the appearance of the doctor radically undermines the notion that romance solves Cléo's problems. Even though Cléo can't manage to find the doctor in his office, he miraculously drives up alongside the bench that Antoine and Cléo are sitting on. He tells them not to worry and he says, "Two months of treatment should put things right. Come and see me tomorrow at eleven to plan the rest." Really this isn't much information, but it does confirm that Cléo has cancer. It doesn't suggest what kind or how severe and so on. From the doctor's response, the spectator might feel that certainly the diagnosis must not be fatal or he wouldn't be so confident. On the other hand, the diagnosis must be serious because he is recommending two months of radiation treatment.

Cléo and Antoine react with concern and confusion. In a shot now famous in French New Wave history, Varda emphasizes their concern through the form of the film in a rapid traveling shot. Varda frames Cléo and Antoine looking concerned at one another as the doctor's car begins to move, and then very quickly the camera backs away from them as if it is connected to the back of the car. In this rapidly moving shot, Cléo and Antoine recede in the distance. Two aspects about this shot hold significant meaning for the film. The fast paced pullback almost prompts a physical response in the spectator since it is quite unusual, even in light of the variety of shots that Varda has employed thus far. It takes the spectator by surprise in the same way that the news takes Cléo by surprise. Additionally, Cléo and Antoine become very small very quickly in the vast frame, which emphasizes the enormity of the news. But this fast paced receding shot also symbolizes the failure of the answer that she just received. The answer was in a sense a non-answer. It was an answer that provided something, but not enough to resolve her doubts one way or another.

This suggests that any answer, no matter how detailed, would always still leave something that is not graspable. That something is the very nature of life and death. No matter how much we reflect on our existence, we cannot find a secure answer to our questions about it. The shot reveals that the doctor's answer is inevitably undermined by the fact that Cléo's questions about her existence, her beauty, and her identity, can't be answered even if she knows when she will or how she will die—or if she knows that she will live. This is the ungraspable aspect of subjectivity that Cléo confronts at the end of the film, and this is what the lack of a substantial answer from the doctor leaves open. But the acknowledgment of this ungraspable aspect of subjectivity is freeing in some way to Cléo.

After the fast pull back, Varda cuts to a tight medium shot of Cléo and Antoine side-by-side looking very nervous. Cléo says, "Why?" But her look of concern dissolves when Antoine says that he is sorry to be leaving and that he'd like to stay with her. Cléo smiles and says that he is there, meaning there with her at that moment. Cléo and Antoine remain together in the moment with the difficult news they are facing. They are strangers each facing uncertainty and possible death—she with a cancer diagnosis and he going back to a war he doesn't believe in—but part of Cléo's relief is the acknowledgment of this uncertainty. At the very end she says, "It seems to me that I'm no longer afraid. It seems to me that I'm happy."[28] The interaction with the doctor and the way the ending is filmed suggest that simply having found Antoine to reassure her of her ideal female beauty is only a small part of this ending. Instead, it is a much more complicated ending.

Cléo seems happy in accepting the tenuousness of her situation, in accepting the uncertainty as a way of existing as a subject. This is very much in keeping with the endings popular in the French New Wave at the time. François Truffaut's *Les Quatre Cents Coups* (*400 Blows*, 1959), for example, follows a troubled young boy who has always dreamt of escaping his problems and going to the ocean. At the end of the film, he does just this, but instead of being a triumphant moment, Truffaut ends the film with a freeze frame of him on the beach looking uncertain, having found neither joy nor suffering in reaching his dream. These endings served to highlight the importance of acknowledging our own existential uncertainty. They also were a direct attack on mainstream narratives that wrapped up all the problems presented in a film with a clear resolution. This lack of a resolution or rather this new kind of ending allowed the filmmakers to present the questioning stance itself as the new awareness at the end of the film. Questioning—or the lack of a resolution—becomes a form of resolution in the French New Wave. This acceptance of questioning over answers is what appears at the end of *Cléo from 5 to 7*.

It's important to point out that Cléo herself may have learned to accept her own questions, but the film does not present her having totally transformed. Her acceptance and enjoyment of Antoine's attention certainly attests to this. Thus, in the end, it is the spectator who might have more awareness after engaging in Cléo's travels and the film's formal interventions, not Cléo herself. Part of the spectator's own awareness comes from engaging the contradictions that Varda nurtures throughout the film. Certainly one of the contradictions is between a feminist awakening (questioning her ideological constraints as well as understanding her own investment in them) and a patriarchal resolution (in which heterosexual romance and ideal female beauty solves everything). The film reveals and holds onto this contradiction until the end and purposely does not provide an answer, except by emphasizing the importance of seeing the contradiction and thus developing an overall questioning stance. This questioning stance is a final feminist gesture. Even if the film doesn't end with a feminist resolution, it remains a feminist film in its devotion to both revealing ideology and keeping a questioning stance rather than providing a comfortable ending. The questioning stance is itself the ultimate feminist position.[29]

Notes

1   Christina Lane's *Feminist Hollywood* provides one example of
     scholarship that investigates the situation of women directors.
     Her book looks at female directors that have moved from
     being independent directors to working within Hollywood.
     As independent female directors, according to Lane, they
     initially developed feminist alternatives to Hollywood but had
     to curtail these concerns and techniques as they moved into
     the Hollywood environment. See Christina Lane, *Feminist
     Hollywood: From Born in Flames to Point Break* (Detroit, MI:
     Wayne State University Press, 2000).

2   Alison Smith, *Agnès Varda* (New York: Manchester University
     Press, 1998), 8.

3   She also comments, "I was naturally involved in fighting
     whatever was prejudicial to women. So we started in France—
     I'm speaking about '48, '49, '50—going with other groups to
     the government, making petitions." Barbara Quart and Agnes
     Varda, "Agnes Varda: A Conversation," *Film Quarterly* 40.2
     (1986–1987): 6.

4   Quart and Varda, "Agnes Varda: A Conversation," 10.

5   In *The Beaches of Agnès*, Varda tells a story about trying to get
     a Hollywood studio to finance her film. She finds and interviews
     the producer who was interested in the film, and he recounts a
     story of Varda slapping a studio executive because the executive
     pinched her cheek. Varda sloughs this off by saying that she is
     not a child and that the issue was who would receive approval
     of the final cut of the film. But it's a revealing story since it
     suggests that Varda believed in being treated as an equal rather
     than being objectified or infantilized. This politically assertive
     side of her personality is not as privileged in her films, in which
     she intends to prompt the spectator into thinking through the
     issues for themselves.

6   In 2015, Agnès Varda received an honorary Palme d'Or at the
     Cannes Film Festival. She is the first female to be awarded this
     honor.

7   Cybelle H. McFadden, *Gendered Frames, Embodied Cameras:
     Varda, Akerman, Cabrera, Calle, and Maiwenn* (Madison, WI:
     Fairleigh Dickinson University Press, 2014), 38.

8 　Ironically, fellow French New Wave director Jean-Luc Godard has a character quote the famous concluding lines from this novel—Patricia proclaims that she prefers "grief to nothing"— in his debut feature film *À bout de souffle* (*Breathless*, 1961).

9 　Interview from 2007 done in her offices and included as an extra on the *La Pointe Courte* DVD.

10 　Interview from 2007 done in her offices and included as an extra on the *La Pointe Courte* DVD.

11 　This is very much the case in her film *The Gleaners and I*. See Hilary Neroni, "Documenting the Gaze: Psychoanalysis and Judith Helfand's *Blue Vinyl* and Agnes Varda's, *The Gleaners and I*," *Quarterly Review of Film and Video* 27.3 (2010): 178–192.

12 　Delphne Bénézet, *The Cinema of Agnès Varda: Resistance and Eclecticism* (New York: Wallflower Press, 2014), 19.

13 　Bénézet's *The Cinema of Agnès Varda* concerns itself with Varda's unique style and approach to filmmaking. She argues that Varda's approach can be understood through its elements of resistance and eclecticism. For Bénézet, this is also a key part of Varda's feminism.

14 　Quoted in Smith, *Agnès Varda*, 6–7.

15 　Feminist theorists have noted this element of femininity from Simone de Beauvoir to bell hooks to Naomi Wolf. See Simone de Beauvoir, *The Second Sex* (New York: Knopf, 1953); bell hooks, *Ain't I a Woman: Black Women and Feminism* (Boston, MA: South End Press, 1981); and Naomi Wolf, *The Beauty Myth* (New York: William Marrow and Company, 1991).

16 　Steven Ungar, *Cléo de 5 à 7* (New York: Palgrave Macmillan, 2008), 57.

17 　The English subtitles of this interior monologue on the Criterion DVD miss the crucial concluding phrase. According to the subtitles, Cléo says, "Don't rush away, pretty butterfly. Ugliness is a kind of death. As long as I'm beautiful, I'm alive." Her comparison to other people simply drops out, and as a result, the viewer fails to grasp the motivation for Cléo's investment in the ideal of female beauty.

18 　Copjec contends that film theory wrongly considers the film screen as a mirror and instead that we should adopt "the more radical insight, whereby the mirror is conceived as a screen." Joan Copjec, *Read My Desire: Lacan Against the Historicists* (Cambridge, MA: MIT Press, 1994), 16.

19   Angela McRobbie, "Young Women and Consumer Culture: An Intervention," *Cultural Studies* 22.5 (September 2008): 542.

20   For more on consumerism as empowerment, see Diane Negra, *What a Girl Wants?: Fantasizing the Reclamation of Self in Postfeminism* (London: Routledge, 2009); Hilary Radner, *Neo-Feminist Cinema: Girly Films, Chick Flicks and Consumer Culture* (New York: Routledge, 2011); Angela McRobbie, *The Aftermath of Feminism: Gender, Culture and Social Change* (New York: Sage, 2012); Yvonne Tasker and Diane Negra, *Interrogating Postfeminism: Gender and the Politics of Popular Culture* (Durham, NC: Duke University Press, 2007); and Sue Thornham, *Women, Feminism and Media* (Edinburgh: Edinburgh University Press, 2007).

21   Smith, *Agnès Varda*, 100.

22   Ungar, *Cléo de 5 à 7*, 65.

23   Smith, *Agnès Varda*, 99.

24   Gerald Peary, "Agnès Varda," *The Real Paper* (Boston, October 15, 1977).

25   Varda does stay true to the concept of the title, however, since the few clocks that are shown throughout the film carefully reflect the proper passage of time.

26   Ungar, *Cléo de 5 à 7*, 41.

27   This early assertion of the film's formal innovative nature also prompts spectator engagement far more than it attempts to set up spectator identification. Varda neither creates a form that totally alienates the spectator from Cléo nor does she try to have the spectator completely identify with Cléo. Instead, she lays out a complex form in which the spectator can engage Cléo, enjoy her, contemplate her, criticize her, and go on her own complicated journey.

28   The English subtitles for the DVD instead reads like this: "My fear seems to be gone. I seem to be happy." While this is a only a slightly different translation from what I have provided ("It seems to me that I'm no longer afraid. It seems to me that I'm happy."), the slight difference in emphasis is significant because it brings out the tenuousness of the statement.

29   One might expand the point and suggest that the basic gestures of the French New Wave and the questioning endings of the films that make up this movement were fundamentally feminist in orientation. It still remains true, however, that Varda's films are the only ones among them that put a female protagonist and female concerns at the center of the narrative.

Conclusion

Wandering through the streets of Paris, Agnès Varda reveals to the spectator her own questions about being a woman. In *Cléo from 5 to 7*, she situates Cléo (Corinne Marchand) in spaces filled with possibility and restriction, asking us to ponder Cléo's arc as a character. In this sense, she also asks the spectator to question a woman's potential path through the social expectations and contradictory ideals they encounter. Varda's questioning stance combined with her innovative formal choices moves the spectator into a feminist place of questioning.

Cléo from 5 to 7 may have come out in 1961, but the themes of the film are still relevant today. Today more than ever how people relate to the image of ideal female beauty is of the utmost importance. The ideology of ideal beauty remains a prevailing ideology, just as women in contemporary society must continue to navigate the opposition between the sex object and the figure of the mother. The ideology of ideal beauty bears on both of these figures because each, the sex object and the mother, has corresponding beauty expectations. Each figure reinforces the idea that women should be, above all else, beautiful, even if their beauty consists in being a perfect mother.

The image of the woman as sex object has determined many cultural trends that remain dominant today—from make-up to skirt lengths to high heels. But the image of the mother has also influenced ideal beauty in the emphasis on purity, flawless skin, and agelessness. Ideal female beauty itself is often an amalgamation of these two contradictory ideals, so that one can even read the demands of female beauty as the site at which contradiction manifests itself. The task of feminist criticism and of feminist film theory is one of adhering to the point of contradiction within femininity and insisting on the intractability of the contradiction. And reading from the point of contradiction is, in fact, what Varda encourages in *Cléo from 5 to 7*.

Every subject exists between looking and being looked at, and every subject must wrestle with this fundamental contradiction of subjectivity. But ideology obscures the contradiction by aligning men with looking and women with being looked at. Feminist film theory draws attention to this ideological obfuscation and encourages us to restore the contradiction of subjectivity to its rightful place. The way that one does this, however, is always complicated and contested, which is why feminist film theory has gone through so many different iterations and why it continues to transform itself even today.

In their pursuit of this fundamental project, feminist film theorists have discovered the importance of developing a questioning stance rather than laying out a strict list of steps that will reach perfection. Each new generation of feminist film theorists have identified filmic techniques and narrative structures that they felt were being used to reinforce patriarchy and others that were employed for feminist purposes. But on each occasion, later feminists have come along to note how the filmic techniques that appeared to reinforce patriarchy actually provided a way of challenging it. Identifying a strict list of dos and don'ts just doesn't work when it comes to the art of film—or any other art for that matter.

Instead of denigrating particular filmic techniques as inherently patriarchal or ideological, the feminist film theorist must examine the relationships between form and content. Any filmic technique, even the most apparently retrograde, can ultimately have a feminist bearing, depending on the relation that it has to the content that it depicts. At the same time, even the most historically revolutionary technique—such as, say, Sergei Eisenstein's dialectical montage—can have a patriarchal function.[1] This is also why we cannot simply condemn a certain filmic content as ideological.

This is in many ways the lesson of the French New Wave in general. The films of the French New Wave did not necessarily have a revolutionary content, but the form of the films forced spectators to engage this content in a way that challenged their ideological preconceptions. This is apparent in the film that serves as the subject of this book. Varda shows Cléo follow a very traditional path—from ignorance and isolation to knowledge and romance—but the way that Varda shows this path undermines its ideological provenance.

The feminist film theorist never simply imposes the claims of feminism indifferently on a recalcitrant film in order to transform the film into an example. The point is rather to engage the relationship that the film establishes between its form and its content. In this way, the feminist film theorist unlocks how film form always involves the question of feminism but never does so in a straightforward or direct way. Feminist film analysis requires the act of interpretation that focuses on relations—between the specific filmic techniques and cultural tropes—and their ability to bring the contradiction of female subjectivity to the fore. The fundamental contradiction of subjectivity is that of looking and being looked at, and it is this contradiction that continues to animate feminist film theory.

All waves of feminism have considered the psychic and material consequence of the ideology that obscures this contradiction, even if they have had different responses to it. Feminist filmmakers—both women and men—shift this dynamic exploring what it means for both women and men to exist within this universal contradiction of looking and being looked at. Feminist filmmakers and film theorists share this attention to the way looking and being looked at as well as the intersections of ideological identities play across the social order.

One of the initial tendencies for each new wave of feminism has been to assume that the lack of progress in society was due to the failures of the previous wave. It is my contention, however, this idea of progress has been hampering feminism. Certainly, to think of feminism in waves is a natural tendency, as we attach modes of feminist thought to particular historical moments. But assuming that the goal of feminism is progress may keep us from engaging ideology in all its manifestations. When we believe we can achieve a final victory over ideological illusion, we succumb to the ultimate ideological illusion. If we imagine that progress will bring us to a time in which feminism is no longer needed, then we will focus on this rather than on the constant need for feminism. We will lose sight of the powerful need for a questioning stance that arises out of the contradictions of subjectivity itself.

Instead, we should see feminism in the way that Walter Benjamin theorized history. In "On the Concept of History," Walter Benjamin conceives the task of the political thinker—to translate into our case, the feminist theorist—to grasp how the struggle of the present is not simply the result of the past but also repeats the revolutionary openings that existed in the past but became closed through history. Benjamin refers to these openings as a "now-time" that disrupts the homogeneous flow of empty time. In the 14th thesis in "On the Concept of History," he makes this point in reference to Robespierre and the French Revolution: "History is the subject of a construction whose site is not homogeneous, empty time, but time filled full by the now-time. Thus, to Robespierre ancient Rome was a past charged with now-time, a past which he blasted out of the continuum of history. The French Revolution viewed itself as Rome reincarnate."[2] That is, each revolution takes part in every revolution of the past, and they exist together not in a series but as repetitions of the same fundamental tendency. For Benjamin, there are constant interruptions in the continuum of history, and these interruptions have an essential link with each other. They are moments when the contradictions of history become evident and disrupt the status quo.

Though each feminist wave responds to different historical conditions, these waves also activate what Benjamin calls the now-time. Rather than seeing progress from one wave to the next, we should see how each takes part in the same struggle, a struggle in which the contradictions surrounding the feminine come to the fore. The goal of feminism is not to create a world in which we no longer need feminism but to create a world that is truly feminist.

Notes

1   See Sergei Eisenstein, *Film Form*, trans. Jay Leyda (New York: Harcourt, Brace, 1949).
2   Walter Benjamin, "On the Concept of History," trans. H. Zohn, in *Selected Writings, Volume 4: 1938–1940* (Cambridge: Harvard University Press, 2003), 395.

FURTHER READING

Simone de Beauvoir, *The Second Sex*, trans. Constance Borde
and Sheila Malovany-Chevallier (New York: Alfred A. Knopf,
2010). The foundational philosophical text of modern feminism.
Beauvoir's book provides a thorough account of the cultural
determinations affecting women and lays the basis for a political
challenge to women's oppression. She also covers the historical
development of patriarchal society and women's place within it.

Joan Copjec, *Read My Desire: Lacan Against the Historicists*
(Cambridge: MIT Press, 1994). Copjec authors the salient
critique of Mulvey's version of feminist film theory. She
articulates a psychoanalytically-informed version of feminism in
this work.

Barbara Creed, *The Monstrous-Feminine: Film, Feminism,
Psychoanalysis* (New York: Routledge, 1993). Through an
examination of a series of horror films, Creed demonstrates how
Hollywood exhibits a horror of the manifestations of the female
body. The book turns to French feminist Julia Kristeva to inform
her interpretation of this phenomenon.

Jennifer Friedlander, *Feminine Look: Sexuation, Spectatorship,
Subversion* (Albany: State University of New York Press, 2008).
Friedlander emphasizes the importance of feminine pleasure.
She examines the relationship between visual representation and
sexual difference, and she uses a series of examples to investigate
how sexual difference itself arises.

bell hooks, *Black Looks: Race and Representation* (Boston: South
End Press, 1992). In this book, hooks reveals the limitations
of earlier feminist film theory by highlighting its failure to take
race into account. She writes in an engaging style and makes her
points through numerous popular examples.

Laura Mulvey, "Visual Pleasure and Narrative Cinema," *Screen* 16.3
(1975): 6–18. The most anthologized essay in the history of film
theory. Mulvey's essay has had an enormous influence on the
field, and all film students should be aware of its central thesis.

Hilary Neroni, *The Violent Woman: Femininity, Narrative, and Violence in Contemporary American Cinema* (Albany: State University of New York Press, 2005). Through an investigation of violent women in the cinema, Neroni exposes the disruptiveness of this figure. She shows that the inability of the violent woman to enter into the standard romantic union evinces this disruptiveness.

Hilary Radner, *Neo-Feminist Cinema: Girly Films, Chick Flicks and Consumer Culture* (New York: Routledge, 2011). Radner provides a critique of cinema and television's role in the emergence of a consumer culture among woman. She locates shows such as *Sex and the City* as neoliberal rather than feminist.

Valerie Smith, *Not Just Race, Not Just Gender: Black Feminist Readings* (New York: Routledge, 1998). An important work in assessing the intersection of race and gender in cinema. She sees how this intersection bears on many different forms of cultural practice.

Patricia White, *Uninvited: Classical Hollywood Cinema and Lesbian Representability* (Bloomington, Indiana: Indiana University Press, 1999). White examines several classical Hollywood films haunted by the specter of lesbian figures. She shows how Hollywood both creates an implicit space for the lesbian spectator while marginalizing her at the same time.

INDEX

Made in the USA
Middletown, DE
19 February 2021